Profitable Part-Time/Full-Time Freelancing

PROFITABLE PART-TIME FULL-TIME FREELANCING

CLAIR REES

Writer's Digest Books — Cincinnati, Ohio

Profitable Part-Time/Full-Time Freelancing. Copyright 1980 by
Clair F. Rees. Printed and bound in the United States of America. All
rights reserved. No part of this book may be reproduced in any form
or by any electronic or mechanical means including information
storage and retrieval systems without permission in writing from the
publisher, except by a reviewer who may quote brief passages in a
review. Published by Writer's Digest Books, 9933 Alliance Road,
Cincinnati, Ohio 45242. First edition.

Library of Congress Cataloging in Publication Data
Rees, Clair F.
    Profitable part-time/full-time freelancing.
    Includes index.
    1. Authorship—Vocational guidance. I. Title.
PN151.R4   808'.025   79-22724
ISBN 0-89879-012-3

To Dixie

CONTENTS

tion books to keep you busy between magazine-article manuscripts, and help you build an increasingly better income.

tions. Your income potential is unlimited, and you have more personal freedom than almost anyone else in town. What you can look forward to when you finally "make it" as a full-time writer.

15. **The Writer and Society (What Will the Neighbors Think?)**
There are some unexpected social adjustments you, your spouse, and the neighbors will have to make when you take up freelancing as a full-time career. A survival guide to coping with public opinion.

This
Writing
Business

Freelance writing offers one of the few great opportunities left for individual freedom, self-expression, and financial gain. In addition, it's a lot of fun and can lead to varying degrees of fame and fortune.

Writing is one of the few totally nondiscriminatory professions. People of any race, sex, size, or age can become successful writers, and you can live on a Wyoming cattle ranch or work from a grass hut in Borneo if that's the lifestyle you prefer. Neither a college degree nor a high school diploma is required for the job. If you enjoy writing—and do it well—you have a highly marketable skill. As long as you're literate and imaginative, and know how to communicate in print, you're a potential freelancer. By definition, you become a professional with that first manuscript sale. But *true* professionalism takes time, hard work, and multiple sales.

Freelancing can be a lucrative part-time pastime that provides both recognition and extra cash; this money-making hobby can eventually form the basis for full-time self-employment. Many part-time freelancers average upwards of $50 an hour for time spent at the typewriter, and a successful full-time professional can earn $40,000, $50,000, or more each year. If you're smart enough and lucky enough to author a best-selling book, you may be well on your way to earning your first million.

Because there are risks involved in making your living entirely from freelance writing, most freelancers are part-time writers who hold down regular nine-to-five jobs but manage to find the time to write for publication. They work at the typewriter evenings and weekends, and many of them earn impressive sums from their freelancing efforts. Part-time freelance writing can provide a respectable second income that may equal or even exceed the wages earned by the writer at his regular job. When that happens, the writer often starts thinking seriously about quitting his employer to take up freelancing on a full-time basis.

While some writers make the change from part-time to full-time freelancing successfully and with few major problems, many aren't psychologically or financially prepared to make the break. These unfortunates become discouraged early in the game, and usually return (or *try* to return) to their old jobs in a matter of months. It's not the lack of writing skill that defeats them, but the lack of knowledge and planning.

This book will show you how to become a successful part-time freelancer. Once you've crossed that threshold and are selling regularly, it will help you evaluate your chances of succeeding as a full-time professional. If you decide those chances are good, the book will help you make the step from part-time to full-time freelance writing as easy and painless as possible.

Right from the beginning, you should realize that part-time freelancing and full-time freelancing are worlds apart. The part-time freelancer takes an entirely different attitude toward this writing business than does the full-time professional who earns his entire living from the typewriter. While a part-time magazine writer may be happy to accept payment after an article is published, the serious professional simply can't work that way. If a magazine doesn't agree to pay promptly on acceptance of an assigned manuscript, that writer will almost never agree to accept the assignment. That points up yet another difference: Most full-time writers will write *only* on assignment—that is, with a firm commitment for the article's purchase—while part-time freelancers are more likely to work "on speculation" in hope of making a sale.

There are other differences as well. The full-time writer has many social, psychological, and financial pressures that the part-time freelancer isn't called upon to bear. True, the self-employed writer is free from a regimented working schedule and *can* lead a perfectly enviable life, but some people find themselves unable to adjust to this kind of freedom. Full-time freelancing *isn't* for everyone, and many writers are happier working on a part-time basis while depending on more conventional employment for the bulk of their income. And that's not to say that the part-time freelancer isn't capable of turning out material that's every bit as professional as that done by a full-time writer. The difference isn't in the quality of writing produced. It's found mainly in the attitude each writer has toward himself, his editors, and his occupation.

In many ways, the part-time freelancer has the best of both worlds: the security and fringe benefits that come with a regular job, and the satisfaction and earning power freelance writing offers. I wrote on a part-time basis for more than nine years before turning to full-time freelancing—and hesitated to take the step even though my part-time writing income (from only a few hours of work each week) had risen to equal the pay I received for a forty-hour week at the office. I recognized that I would be giving up much more than the comfort of a regular salary when I quit my job. There are important fringe benefits like health insurance and retirement pensions that you take for granted when you're working for a large corporation. When you become self-employed, you have to earn enough money to provide your own medical insurance coverage and retirement fund, and this gets expensive when you can't take advantage of group rates. What's more, there are no such things as paid vacation and sick leave for a freelance writer. When you're not working, the money stops coming in—it's as simple as that.

In addition, it's difficult—if not downright impossible—for

a full-time freelancer to stabilize his or her cash flow. You can guarantee yourself a certain regular monthly income by becoming a magazine or newspaper columnist, and you'll probably be getting regular assignments from certain editors by the time you decide to make the step to full-time freelancing. But by and large your income will fluctuate greatly from one month to the next. Unless you've planned properly and set some money aside to help ease you through the low times, a "steak or beans" income can quickly destroy a promising freelance career. Worrying about unpaid bills doesn't much help a writer's creativity; too much anxiety can bring on a monumental case of writer's block and may eventually lead to more serious health problems. If you're not temperamentally suited to the insecurity each writer must face when starting out as a full-time freelancer, you'll probably be much happier (and more relaxed) writing on a part-time basis. There are many respected professionals in the business who have no intention of giving up the security of regular nine-to-five employment to freelance full-time.

Some writers who *have* made the break to full-time self-employment have soon become disenchanted with their new-found profession. These unhappy freelancers would gladly give up the glory to return to the security of a salaried job—if they could find one that paid enough or that wouldn't be too confining. Giving up regular employment isn't easy, but the return route can be even more difficult and hazardous. I tried to return to the corporate fold after my first year of freelancing, but resigned before the week was out. It's tough to accept seemingly meaningless office routine after being your own boss for just a few months. You fret through time-wasting conferences where nothing much happens but the airing of corporate egos, and the idea of punching a time clock or even keeping regular office hours becomes suddenly repugnant. Full-time freelancing can literally ruin your worth to a conventional business organization.

Of course, there are many real advantages to freelancing full-time. For those who plan ahead and properly prepare themselves for the switch to self-employment, full-time freelancing can be a thoroughly enjoyable new world. And if you've done things right, it can be a highly lucrative world as well.

One of the genuine benefits of being a self-employed writer is that you're able to choose the kinds of assignments you're truly interested in—and working at something that has your undivided interest is a lot more fun than carrying out some ho-hum task your boss has given you. There's also the realization that your success or failure depends entirely on you. What's more, the sky's the limit. While you had a certain amount of security as a salaried corporate employee, chances are that salary increased just enough each year to keep you slightly ahead of the rising cost of living. Even those well-earned promotions probably didn't bring you more than a few thousand extra dollars of increased annual income. In short, your earnings were limited to lock-step increases in a particular salary scale, and only freelancing or some other form of moonlighting could help you substantially better your standard of living.

While it's always possible to fail as a full-time freelancer, it's also possible to increase your income considerably in a relatively short time. In my first full year of self-employment as a writer, I managed to earn just slightly more than I had the year before as public relations manager of a manufacturing concern. But I was able to nearly *double* that income the following year. The rewards of success can be sweet.

Another point that shouldn't be overlooked is that while regular corporate employment provides a certain amount of security, a successful freelancer actually enjoys even more job security. We all know of people who have lost long-standing jobs through a variety of circumstances—reduction in force when sales are down, a personality clash with a new supervisor, reorganization due to a merger—and some of us have been laid off or fired ourselves. As a freelance writer, you're not dependent on the fortunes and foibles of a single business organization. You have many different clients, and if one or two of them go out of business or "fire" you for some reason or another, you always have the others to fall back on. There are literally thousands of magazine- and book-publishing firms you can write for, so you're never at a loss for potential clients. Your success—or failure—as a writer depends on you, and you alone.

Freelance writing offers many rewards, whether you do it on a part-time or full-time basis. This book will show you how to make your writing career a successful one.

Part-Time Freelancing: How to Begin

How do you decide whether or not you have what it takes to be a freelance writer? Anyone who puts words on paper can call himself a writer and I know many people who do just that. But before you can legitimately call yourself a *professional* writer you have to be able to sell those words and see them published.

Even if you've already made the grade as a professional writer, you may not be able to hack it as a freelancer. Newspaper reporters, advertising copywriters, and public relations practitioners qualify as writing professionals, but the work they do is much less demanding than that which freelancers are called upon to perform. Such salaried scribes serve the same masters day after day, and start each day with a pretty good idea of what the boss expects. The prose they produce will be tightly tailored to particular specifications, and if the first draft fails to please there's usually the chance to do it over and over until it does.

The freelance writer who hawks his or her wares in the national magazine/book publishing markets first must sell a story or book idea to an editor halfway across the country—and then produce a finished piece of writing that can compete effectively with the multiple thousands of other submissions editors see each year. The piece must be exactly right the first time around, and each editor has his own idea of how a subject should be handled.

To be successful, a freelance writer needs other important skills besides being able to entertain or inform in print. Freelancing is a business, and to make a go of it you need a certain amount of business sense. Full-time professionals must be salesmen, bookkeepers, and hard-eyed negotiators. They need a surprising amount of self-discipline, including the ability to stretch a buck between irregular paydays. Writing ability is only one requirement, even though it's the most basic of the bunch.

Fortunately, few freelancers begin their writing careers on a full-time basis. The majority of magazine writers and book authors first take up freelancing part-time and depend on more traditional nine-to-five employment for rent and groceries. That means they can pay less attention to the business of freelancing while learning the basics of the trade and developing important editorial contacts. As a matter of fact, only a small percentage of all freelance writers—including those who sell regularly to national markets—work full-time at the profession.

Many people claim the desire to become freelance writers, but few ever act on this impulse. It takes a certain amount of self-confidence to submit that very first manuscript, and if it returns to your mailbox with a printed rejection form, it's even harder to send out a second time. Egos are fragile things, and the fear of rejection is undoubtedly the reason more would-be freelancers fail to take the plunge.

I know several now-successful writers who took years to build up confidence to the point where they actually put that first submission in the mail. One good friend of mine didn't believe he could compete with professional writers because he lacked professional training himself. He had a college degree, but because it wasn't in English or journalism he didn't feel his writing skills were polished enough to communicate effectively. I talked him out of that notion, and he now sells nearly everything he writes. Another acquaintance never bothered to finish high school, but didn't let the absence of a formal education stop him from becoming a successful free-lancer.

The fact is, no editor is going to ask to see your academic credentials when you submit an idea or a finished article. He couldn't care less how many college degrees you have—or don't have—as long as your writing is clear, easy to read, and reasonably entertaining. As a matter of fact, it's possible to let a literary education come between you and potential sales. You use considerably different language when writing to impress a professor of English literature than you use in everyday communication. Trying to impress an editor with the vocabulary and high-blown phraseology you learned as a liberal arts undergraduate is a real mistake when selling to the popular market.

What kinds of skill and training do you really need to become a successful freelancer? How are these skills best acquired, and how can you evaluate your own proficiency as a writer before you send out that first submission? How can you tell if you're suited for this writing business? And finally, how do you begin?

Good writing is something that can be learned, but never taught effectively. The *mechanics*—sentence structure, grammar, punctuation—can be taught in the classroom, but the ability to produce an interesting—and salable—manuscript with these basic communication tools is something that must come from within.

Every successful writer I know is a compulsive reader, and I suspect this is true of every good writer throughout the ages. Unless you honestly like to read, and enjoy it to the point of addiction, I doubt the writing life is for you. A voracious appetite for the printed word is the one thing you can count on to give you a real feel for writing. Regular readers develop an instinctive feel for grammar and sentence structure, and their initial writing style will be an amalgam of everything they've read.

Nonreaders lack this important leg-up, and have a difficult time developing a real writing style. You can be taught proper punctuation and the relationship between nouns and verbs, but unless you read a lot you'll never be comfortable putting your own thoughts on paper.

The honest love of reading is more important to a writer than a whole trunkful of college diplomas. That's not to say that advanced education isn't valuable to a freelancer. Any English course will help polish your prose, and the report writing required in most college classrooms can be a real plus. The university experience helps you organize your thoughts and can make you better informed in many different areas. In addition, a four-year degree is the union card needed for almost any white-collar job these days, and you'll need some kind of decent employment to keep you financially afloat while freelancing part-time.

In other words, the more you can learn, the better writer you're likely to be. At the same time, you should recognize that there are other "classrooms" than those found on a university campus. Any work experience can give you a background to draw on when you're sitting at the typewriter. The roughest blue-collar job can provide the basis for an exciting novel, and many successful literary careers have been launched by ex-longshoremen, oil-rig roustabouts, and other action-oriented workers.

If you already have a job you're satisfied with, don't feel you have to give it up to obtain a college education before you can start writing for publication. The same advice goes for homemakers with spare time on their hands. At this point, you're better off spending your time writing than trying to further your formal education.

If you have what it takes to be a writer, chances are you're already trying your hand at it. Even if you haven't yet attempted publication, you've undoubtedly written short pieces simply for your own satisfaction and may have put in a stint on your school or neighborhood newspaper. Any writing you do is good practice; there's no substitute for sitting behind a typewriter to make you better at stringing words together.

However, there's a big difference between simply writing for personal enjoyment and producing marketable material. To do the former, the only one you have to please is yourself—

and we all know what a pushover you can be! Letting friends and relatives read your output is no good, either, unless they happen to be English teachers, editors, or professional writers themselves. The true test of writing ability comes in the marketplace. If editors are willing to spend good money to buy a manuscript, you know it's good—maybe not *great*, but at least publishable. Only when this happens can you call yourself a real writer or professional.

Before you start marketing your writing wares, it's important to establish some professional goals. Typically, the unpublished beginner thinks only of breaking into print. Getting that first byline is an important step which boosts shaky self-esteem. However, you should look beyond that first sale right from the beginning. Anyone with a smidgen of writing ability can sell manuscripts if he or she is willing to send them to the lowest-paying pulp magazines, where remuneration—if and when it comes—may only be complimentary copies of the publication itself. Some writers advocate giving your work away free if that's what it takes to get published, but I'm not one of them! Being paid in contributor's copies is the poorest way I know to begin a writing career. If your work is good enough to merit publishing at all, it should be good enough to rate financial reward. No professional works without receiving a fee, and if your goal is to become a truly professional writer you must never fall into the trap of vanity payments.

In some ways, a professional writer is much like an attorney or physician first starting out. Would you trust a surgeon who offered to remove your appendix gratis because he "needed the practice" and wanted word to get around that he could handle the chore? How would you feel about letting a lawyer defend you in a potentially costly suit if he declined payment because he was so inexperienced? Offering your work without charge to a reputable editor will bring the same response. You should never advertise that you're a rank beginner, and the surest way to do just that is to indicate your willingness to accept lower than standard payment.

If your long-range writing goals include earning a fair portion of your income from the typewriter and maybe some day freelancing full-time, you should consider submitting to the highest-paying markets right from the start. It's a better-than-even chance that those first few submissions will be returned, so you should steel yourself against initial rejections and promptly resubmit the manuscripts to less prestigious publications where the odds are usually better. However, if you've chosen the right subject and have done a good job of tailoring the manuscript to that high-priced market, you could be pleasantly surprised. Several years ago an aspiring outdoor writer telephoned me long distance for advice. He was just starting out and had sold his first four manuscripts to *Field & Stream* on first attempt. Now he was trying to branch out a bit, and wanted suggestions about selling to magazines offering much lower rates. Even after succeeding with one of the top-paying publishers in his field—not once, but four times running—he didn't think of himself as a true professional, and lacked the confidence to try other top magazines.

You may have to serve your apprenticeship building sales at magazines with circulations that fall short of the multi-million-copy sales of the glamor publications, but never hesitate to try your luck at the top if you have something you think is right for that market. The sooner you start thinking of yourself as a writing *professional*, the better. And a professional freelancer always shoots for the top dollar possible. Remember, too, that there's a first time for everything—even the superstars of the profession had to sell their first manuscripts to some flinty-eyed editors who'd never heard of them.

Your long-range goal may be becoming a novelist rather than a contributor of nonfiction magazine-length manuscripts. A novel requires a much greater expenditure of time and energy than writing a two-thousand-word piece for the periodicals, and nearly all first novels must be sold as a completed package. Until you've proven yourself in this demanding field, you must work entirely on speculation—which means you have no commitment from an editor to buy. That situation is one most professional writers try to avoid, but until you actually sell one or two novels there's not much you can do about it. If you want to test your ability by selling a few short stories first, there are a number of magazines that still buy short fiction, although this market has shrunk considerably in recent years.

The beginning novelist is pretty much at the mercy of the publishers he submits his work to. First novels rarely make much money for either author or publisher, and so have a hard time in the marketplace. However, there are certainly exceptions to this rule, and this is one reason publishers continue to buy first novels. Another is the recognition that subsequent works by an author tend to bring more respectable financial returns, so the publisher may be willing to gamble on a first novel as a long-range investment.

If you're dead set on becoming a novelist and writing for magazines bores you, by all means expend your energies authoring that novel. There's no point wasting time on projects that won't directly help you reach your goal.

Nonfiction books represent another excellent market for the freelancer. The demand is high for good how-to books, and you don't have to worry about characterization, setting, and dialogue. Unlike a first novel, it's possible to sell book-length nonfiction on the basis of a query letter and short proposal. Nearly all successful freelancers turn out nonfiction books from time to time, and the steady—if not always impressive—royalties these projects bring form an important part of the full-timer's income.

A stint at magazine writing is excellent training for that initial nonfiction book. In addition to helping you become more familiar with your subject, writing a series of short articles—and then having them published—gives you needed credence when you propose your book to a nonfiction editor. This kind of preparation also gives you a pretty good idea of your capabilities as a writer, and as you begin selling regularly to magazines your confidence increases.

Freelancers begin magazine writing for several different reasons. In the first place, editorial response is usually much faster, and positive reinforcement is vitally needed at this stage. Being much shorter than book-length manuscripts, magazine articles take considerably less time to prepare, and consequently, you can—and should—have several circulating at once. A "no thanks" is less devastating when you have other submissions in the works and when it comes in response to a project you've spent only a few hours on, rather than months or years.

There are thousands of magazines being published monthly, and this creates an enormous demand for well-written freelance material. If you have any potential at all to become a professional writer, you should be able to tap this hungry market in short order. I'll tell you how in chapter 3.

Unfortunately, writing ability alone—pure talent—isn't sufficient to make you a successful freelancer. The one quality dividing real professionals from most would-be writers is discipline. If you can write only when the Muse is smiling you're not likely to get far in the profession. Manuscripts are sold by people who have the grit to sit at the typewriter—and stay there—until an assignment is finished and ready for mailing. Waiting until you're "in the mood" to write is a luxury the professional freelancer simply can't afford.

Many people romanticize the writer's trade and some beginners labor under serious misconceptions regarding the lifestyle of a full-time freelancer. Since I became a full-time writer, I've worked harder than I ever did as a corporate employee. The hours are usually longer than you'd like them to be, and you're subject to the problems any businessman falls prey to. There are both risks and rewards—even long-time professionals get rejection slips now and then, and a magazine can go bust still owing you money. You can have dry spells in which the bank account drops steadily lower despite the fact you're hard at work, and doubts can creep in to undermine your will and confidence.

On the other hand, a freelancer enjoys an amount of personal freedom shared by few others, and if he's successful, his income can soar. For people who honestly enjoy writing, there's no finer way to make a living.

In addition to offering the potential for an above-average income doing exactly what you like, freelancing has other, less tangible rewards. Every writer has enough ego to enjoy seeing his name in print, and the first time you're asked to autograph a book or magazine article you've authored can be a real thrill. Writing professionally can give you a deep sense of accomplishment. You can see what you've produced when your work hits print, and even bask in a few moments of quiet self-congratulation. Contrast this situation with that of the factory hand or office worker who enjoys no real sense of identity with what he does.

I've mentioned that writing discipline is a necessary ingredient of any professional freelancer's makeup. This is a matter of simple fact, but don't despair if you haven't yet mastered the ability to pound out prose when you don't feel like it. This comes only through practice and dogged determination. No one is born with the talent to work when he doesn't really want to; the fact that good writing is a creative act doesn't make the job easier. Part-time freelancers build discipline with each succeeding sale, and soon learn to set a certain time aside each day to finish those assignments on time.

Freelancing husbands and wives usually find that it's easier to take an hour or so first thing in the morning, or wait until the children are in bed at night, to turn to the typewriter. You must avoid interruptions if anything is to be accomplished, and writing discipline develops as you program yourself to take full advantage of these time periods.

Most part-time freelancers follow a regular writing schedule that may give them only an hour a day; however, an hour of serious writing can produce a surprising amount of salable material each year if that hour is faithfully used each and every day.

Full-time writers may spend only four or five hours a day actually writing, but that much honest concentration can yield big dividends. A typical office employee is at his desk a full eight hours or more, but much of that time is spent socializing, taking coffee breaks, daydreaming, or otherwise wasting productive time. When you take into account the multiple meetings he attends, the phone calls he makes, and the various other nonproductive things he does in the course of the day, it's easy to see why an efficient freelancer can generate more money while spending less time at work.

Again, discipline is the key. The writer *can't* waste too much time at nonproductive chores or he'll soon be out of business. If he allows himself to be distracted by phone calls, television programs, or the sudden urge to build a sandwich, those deadlines won't be met and the checks will quit coming in. A writer who sets five hours of writing as a daily minimum must spend all five of those hours seated at the typewriter with his fingers on the keys. Discipline is something you have to work at all the time, and should be a prime goal of the beginning or part-time freelancer. If you can't develop a regular writing discipline, you'll never be able to earn much of a living as a freelancer.

What kind of attitude, training, and skills do you need to become a successful freelance writer? If you honestly enjoy writing enough to do it on a daily basis, you've got the biggest essential licked. Grammar and punctuation skills can be learned in the classroom or through a lifetime of recreational reading, while the only effective way to train yourself to write is to sit at a desk and do just that. Learning to write well enough to sell your work regularly may come easy to you, or it may take a fair amount of trial-and-error struggle. The one thing I'm sure of is that if you really *want* to be a freelance writer and are willing to work at it, you're almost certain to enjoy some success. Whether you can make a full-time living at it, only time and your editors will tell. Even if you're not temperamentally suited to full-time freelancing, part-time writing offers its own rewards. If you lack the drive or ability to become one of the superstars of the game, you may still be able to substantially supplement the earnings from your regular job.

Not everyone is cut out to be a professional writer, and some who try may be wasting their time. But the only way to find out if you have the basic ability to communicate in print is to give it a try. As far as I'm concerned, it's well worth the gamble; potential rewards far outweigh the risks involved. If you don't succeed at first, don't quit too soon. The final essential for writing success is a skin six inches thick. Editors are only human, and rejection notices shouldn't be taken too seriously—at least at first. When you're starting out, don't be put off by a dozen or so rejection slips. A surprising number of highly successful writers have begun by collecting drawersful of "no thanks" notes, but kept trying.

If you really want to be a writer, chances are you have a fair amount of writing aptitude. While there are exceptions, we tend to enjoy most the things we're good at. If putting words down on paper came hard to you, you probably wouldn't be reading this book. The fact that you bothered to buy (or borrow) it in the first place shows that you have an above-average interest in freelancing.

Do you have what it takes to be a freelance writer? Very probably you do. It all depends on what goals you have and how determined you are to reach them.

Making
That First
Magazine
Sale

The toughest part of any undertaking is simply getting started, and the biggest stumbling block the beginning freelancer faces is that first sale. That's what separates the professional from the would-be writer: cash in exchange for a publishable manuscript.

Fortunately, getting published isn't as difficult as many new writers think it's going to be. If you're serious and willing to do the necessary work, that stumbling block is mostly imaginary. The more quickly you overcome it, the sooner you'll start earning the rewards of a freelance writing career.

Most magazine queries or article attempts fail because the writer isn't honestly familiar with the publication he or she is trying to sell to. This violates the first cardinal rule of freelancing: Know your market.

You should never submit anything—not even a query—to a magazine you haven't read and studied. Simply skimming the table of contents and reading one or two articles won't do. You should thoroughly examine a half-dozen recent issues and critically dissect several articles in each. You're trying to learn exactly what kinds of articles that magazine publishes, and how the editor likes them slanted.

Does the editor want a writer's opinion, or does he print only documented facts? What about style? Are the articles written in third person only, or is first-person voice often used? How much dialogue appears in each feature? Are anecdotes used extensively, or does the copy reflect straight journalistic reportage? Are the articles strictly service-oriented with emphasis on "how-to," or does sheer entertainment appear as the dominant theme?

What audience is the editor trying to reach? You need to know who's buying the magazine before you can intelligently determine how to slant your writing. The quickest way to mine this valuable information is to study the advertising that appears in the publication. Are the ads oriented toward housewives or hobbyists, hunters or health faddists? If you're dealing with a specialty magazine catering to a narrowly defined readership, this will be immediately obvious. However, some publications aim for—and attract—a wide variety of readers. Studying the ads should tell you quite a bit about the average reader's age and economic status, as well as his or her leisure interests. Pick up a magazine and carefully look through it. If you find full-page advertisements for expensive sports cars, that tells you a fair percentage of the readers are affluent enough to afford this kind of transportation. It also tells you something about the probable age bracket the magazine appeals to and may indicate a heavily male readership. Take a look at the people shown in the ad—are they young, sparkling, and bursting with energy? Or do a majority of the layouts depict mature adults? Notice the clothing ads. Are they selling Levi's and other casual attire, or high-fashion furs and tuxedos?

You need all this information, and more. The better you can define your audience, the better your chance of connecting with an on-the-mark query or manuscript.

In addition to giving you a good understanding of readership demographics, such a detailed study of the magazine can quickly let you know if a piece too similar to the one you have in mind has already seen print. While certain topics are covered periodically in some magazines, most publications won't be interested in a subject they've featured within the past two years or so. Similarly, an editor may shy away from an idea recently used by a competing publication. If you submit an article or query about a subject featured just last month by the magazine you're trying to sell to, you've not only wasted your own valuable time—you've also admitted to the editor you haven't done your homework, and that you're really not all that familiar with his publication. This isn't a sin, but it certainly ranks as a freelancing faux pas.

One way to determine if your idea has already been used is to check the *Reader's Guide to Periodical Literature* at your local public library. If the magazine you're interested in isn't listed here (and many aren't), the library may have back issues of the publication on hand. Some magazines publish annual indexes, which usually appear in the January issue and list articles published the preceding year.

This study-your-market technique is basic to any magazine sale, but it is critical for that very first attempt. For this reason, your first approach should be directed toward a publication you yourself read regularly. This will put you on familiar ground, and if you subscribe to that magazine you'll already know what subjects have recently been printed and therefore aren't likely to interest the editor. Even more important, you likely have a good deal of interest in the subject matter covered by the publication—otherwise, you wouldn't be reading it month after month. It's much easier to produce a good article about something you're honestly interested in than to crank out a salable manuscript simply for the payment involved. Not that money can't be an acceptable motivator—full-time professionals often find themselves accepting assignments they wouldn't normally consider simply because a healthy amount of cash is offered in return. But while you're getting your writing feet on the ground, you'll be far better off choosing only subjects you can get excited about. This enthusiasm is nearly always reflected in the manuscripts you turn in, and is an obvious plus.

How do you come up with salable ideas? If you've got an ounce of creative fluid in your veins, that problem is easy to solve. Experienced freelancers always have more ideas at hand than they can possibly use, simply because new ideas constantly suggest themselves. Once you've trained yourself to think like a writer, you'll be able to come up with at least a half-dozen viable subjects every time you put your mind to it, and your subconscious will be storing fresh article ideas away on a continuous basis. If the beginning writer has a difficult time coming up with article inspirations, it's probably because he's trying too hard.

The best approach I've found on those rare occasions when I need to think of something new to write about is to relax and thumb through a few issues of some of my favorite magazines. Then I stop and think about activities I've planned for the near future. Usually, something clicks along about this point and I have a new article idea at hand.

As you begin to think like a writer—that is, become increasingly aware of what interests readers—article ideas are likely to pop into your head any time, day or night. Many writers carry pocket notebooks wherever they go and jot thoughts down immediately as they occur. Unless these thoughts are preserved on paper, they'll likely disappear before you're ready to work on them.

A number of successful freelancers maintain extensive files of newspaper clippings, jotted notes, odd statistics, and a thousand and one other things that may one day be useful in a book or magazine article. I must confess I no longer do this— I've learned from experience that once something is filed away, I promptly forget about it. Bits and pieces of unrelated information only clutter my office, and if I don't get around to incorporating the data in an article query or book proposal within a couple of weeks, I simply throw it out. I've found that if I don't act on an idea within that length of time, I probably never will. Many writers find such catchall filing systems helpful, though, and they're certainly worth trying.

There are dozens of different ways to court the Muse. Editors like to buy fresh slants on old ideas, so if you can think of a new approach even overworked subjects can be made attractive. How-to articles are always in demand, and if you have a particular expertise, you can usually find a magazine interested in mining your experience. Service magazines like to print articles that will help their readers do things better, faster, or cheaper. Other publications are more concerned with people than things, and personal interviews with experts, entertainers, or politicians are the key to fast sales.

If you have what you think is a good idea for an article but don't know where to sell it, check the listings in *Writer's Market*. This volume, published annually by Writer's Digest Books, is a comprehensive compilation of both book and periodical publishers, the latter grouped according to interest. Once you've discovered a few magazines that look like potential purchasers of your proposed manuscript, take a trip to the newsstand and try to locate some current issues. If there are none available, write to the editor, using the address listed in *Writer's Market*. Some publishers send free sample copies to possible contributors, while others charge the newsstand price, plus postage. Many magazines offer style sheets and other writer's guidelines, and you should request these as well.

However you go about it, get your hands on some copies of the magazine before you try to sell anything to it. Remember that first rule: Know your market. It's impossible to learn what a magazine is likely to buy without reading it first. Querying an editor cold without studying the publication, or submitting a manuscript blind "over the transom," is both unprofessional and foolish. It's usually a waste of time, and while you may have extra hours or minutes to fritter away I can guarantee you the editor won't. An obviously unsuitable manuscript or query directed to a busy editor won't enhance your possibilities for future sales to her.

Magazines can be divided roughly into two categories, based on size of circulation and the amount of money they're willing to pay for manuscripts. On the one hand you have the large-circulation, prestige periodicals. These publications often pay well, with a feature article bringing $1000 or more—sometimes considerably more. Payment is nearly always made on acceptance, which means a check should arrive within a month or so after the editor decides to purchase your piece. Another plus is that many more people will read your article once it sees print, and it certainly does a writer's career no harm to have her byline appear in the big-circulation slicks (so called because the magazine is printed on high-grade, glossy paper).

At the other extreme are the small-circulation specialty magazines. These usually cater to a narrowly defined audience, and the circulation is a tiny fraction of that boasted by the prestige publications. Pay schedules are much lower here, and chances are good that payment will be made only after the magazine has been published and placed on the newsstand. This means that it may be a year or more before you see your money, and since editors have a penchant for rescheduling articles without bothering to notify the author in advance, that check you expected with publication of the November issue may not materialize in your mailbox until the following May. Payment on publication isn't a desirable state of affairs for even a part-time freelancer, but when you're just starting out you may be forced to accept it in order to sell.

It obviously would be nice to make that very first sale to one of the large-circulation, quality magazines. The money shows up sooner, and when it arrives the check is usually larger. Such magazines are also a more satisfying showcase for your work. So why not start at the top?

Why not, indeed? Remember the beginning writer I mentioned earlier—who, incidentally, had no college or professional training—who sold his first four manuscripts to one of the top-paying outdoor magazines? The checks he received were substantial, and he envisioned quitting his regular job as a railroad brakeman to work full-time at the typewriter. The last I heard he was still with the railroad, although I see his byline every now and then—still in the big-circulation magazines. I know on occasion he gets a rejection slip instead of a fat check, but for the most part he's been consistently successful selling his work to the most desirable markets in his chosen specialty.

If he'd lacked the nerve to try the big-name publications right at the beginning, he would probably have been successful selling manuscripts to some smaller magazine at much poorer pay. Eventually he would have graduated to the large-circulation magazines, but he short-circuited this more traditional approach by starting at the top. In his case, it paid off. It could just as easily pay off for you.

The danger in submitting those first, fledgling articles to the well-known, better-paying periodicals is that the competition can be terrific. These are the publications every writer hopes to sell to, and the number of unsolicited manuscripts received in some editorial offices routinely reaches several hundred each month. Considering that some of these magazines buy only one or two freelance manuscripts in this time span, your odds of making a sale can be fewer than one in a hundred. When you compete for those four-figure paychecks, you have to know that the chance of rejection is greater than when you choose to play in a lower-paying market.

Actually, the odds aren't as bad as they sound, particularly if you've done your homework and carefully analyzed what the magazine is publishing. Many of the "over-the-transom," or unsolicited, manuscripts will be far wide of the mark as far as the editor's needs or tastes are concerned. A good percentage of the editorial slush pile will be made up of unprofessionally prepared pieces that have no hope of getting beyond the first reader, and many of the other submissions will contain various flaws that make them unsuitable for publication—poor-quality photos, glaring inaccuracies, or a presentation slanted toward the wrong audience.

Still, even old hands with hundreds of published articles to their credit expect to get turned down now and then when submitting to the top markets. The competition is stiff, even when you discount a good share of the editorial offerings as obvious rejects. Since you've studied the magazine and prepared a professional-looking manuscript, your submission won't fall into this unfortunate category. However, you must realistically appraise your chances of success. When you compete with top professionals, you can't allow yourself to become discouraged if your manuscript bounces back with a printed rejection form. The higher the stakes, the greater the odds are likely to be against you. That doesn't mean you shouldn't play. As long as you realize that you're likely to strike out a few times before you connect with the more prestigious periodicals, there's no reason at all not to try your hand at this market. And that means right from the first. Do your best, be persistent, and don't allow rejection slips to discourage you. You need a fairly thick skin to submit to the best-paying magazines as an unpublished beginner. But the rewards can make it worthwhile.

If you're like most new writers, you'll be more anxious about simply making that first sale than getting top dollar for your manuscript. Creative egos tend to be fragile, and the majority of beginners hunger for at least some degree of early success.

If the prospect of receiving a few rejection slips truly bothers you, you should probably lower your sights a bit. This means sending your first submissions to the smaller magazines, where both pay and prestige may be lower—and where you hope the competition isn't as fierce.

These less famous publications range from regional magazines to hobby, homemaking, and how-to publications. Almost every kind of business in this country has one or more trade magazines catering to people in that particular industry, and this is a highly receptive market for well-written freelance material. The range of specialty publications being printed is almost unbelievable, and if you have above-average (or even only average) knowledge of anything from guns to golf, you can probably find a magazine eagerly looking for someone with such expertise. Even if you lack technical knowledge about a subject, don't discount the possibility of selling to this market. The ability to research is a basic writing tool, and if you find a subject that interests you it's relatively easy to learn enough about it to write salable articles.

In many cases, the pay isn't all that bad. And while many of these smaller-circulation magazines pay on publication, there are others who pay promptly on acceptance. You'll still have competition to contend with, but it's generally much less intense.

In other words, a well-thought-out, properly researched, and professionally written piece has an even better chance of being accepted by an editor of a specialty magazine than it would have at one of the large-circulation magazines. It's a simple matter of statistics—where fewer submissions are sent, the odds of acceptance automatically go up.

Regardless of whether you submit to the large-circulation publications or the specialty magazines, you need to make your presentation as professional as possible. Study several back issues to learn as much as possible about each particular market. Then think of a subject—and treatment—that should capture the editor's interest.

While we're on the subject of article treatments, don't overlook the possibility of reworking the same basic article idea, tailoring it to a number of noncompeting markets. For example, a story about a new energy-saving invention could contain enough information to make it salable to several different magazines. A general article about the new development and its possible impact on consumers could be written for *Parade*, while a similar, possibly more technical piece could go to *Popular Science* or *Mechanix Illustrated*. A regional magazine or local newspaper may want a story about the inventor himself, and if his invention attracts enough publicity *People Weekly* would become a potential market. If a subject is interesting enough to generate a single article sale, chances are you can multiply your earnings by rewriting it with different slants for other markets, as well.

Once you reach this point, you can either go ahead and write the article and send it off, or write a query letter to check on the editor's possible interest. There are two schools of thought regarding which approach is best. An editor isn't likely to give you—or any writer—a firm assignment based on a query alone unless you've sold to him before or he's read enough of your work in other magazines to have faith in your ability to do the job right. So even an attractive query won't bring you more than a tentative go-ahead. If the editor likes your idea, he'll ask you to send it along "on spec." That way, he's not committing himself to buy until after he's seen the completed article. But at least you know he's interested in the basic idea, and an assignment submitted after an editor's go-ahead stands an excellent chance of eventually being accepted. Even when the editor has specified that the article is to be considered as a speculative piece, his green light is tantamount to an agreement to buy if the manuscript meets editorial specifications. In other words, if you do a good job the article will sell.

Obviously, if you already have an article written and ready for mailing, sending a query letter is a waste of time. A finished manuscript is much easier to judge than a letter promising to write it, and the editor can give you a definite yes or no by return mail. You don't need a sales letter if you can put the finished product in an editor's hand.

Too, there are some kinds of writing that can be difficult to presell via the query-letter approach. Humor falls into this category, so if you're trying to find a publisher for something funny you'd be well advised to simply put the manuscript in the mail. If the editor appreciates your sense of humor and it's the type of piece he can run, he'll probably buy. On the other hand, if you'd told him in a query letter that you had an incredibly hilarious piece of writing to sell him, chances are he would have discouraged the submission. Humor is difficult to produce, and is best judged after the fact. Editors know this, and rather than take your word for your ability to pen witticisms, they invariably want to see for themselves. Other articles that should probably be submitted as completed manuscripts include opinion and commentary pieces, editorials, and book reviews. All fiction falls into the same category.

My own feeling is that querying is the more professional approach for most types of articles, and makes good sense for several reasons. In the first place, you're able to establish several important facts before you spend a lot of time researching and writing the proposed article. The idea you have may be an excellent one but may not be right for the magazine at just that time. The editor may already have purchased a similar piece or exhausted his annual budget for buying freelance articles. There may be a planned change in the magazine's editorial thrust that could drastically change future content. If the magazine can't—or won't—use the manuscript for one reason or another, there's not much point in writing and submitting it.

If the editor admits your idea has possibilities and gives you permission to submit it "on speculation," you have a real jump on the competition. For starters, you know that if you keep your end of the bargain by producing an interesting, competently written piece, there's a good chance it will sell. In the second place, when your manuscript arrives at the editorial office with your covering letter that says in effect, "Here's the assignment you wanted to see," it bypasses the first and second readers and goes directly to the editor's desk. Some editors ask you to include their go-ahead letter with your submission to make sure this is what actually happens. They've authorized the effort, and they want to make sure they get to see it. The advantage here is obvious. Instead of being required to please one, two, or even three other people before your copy reaches the only person who has authority to buy, you only have to pass muster with that lone individual. The preliminary readers are charged with winnowing out the chaff to save the editor's valuable time. In other words, they return a lot of stuff that the editor never even lays eyes on. If one of these individuals has a bad day, your perfectly good submission may be the victim of a moment's bad temper. Or a first reader may find objections that the editor wouldn't. Whatever the reasons, a manuscript reviewed by a single person (the boss) has a much greater chance of being accepted than one that must first run the gauntlet of lesser editors.

Another thing you have going for you when you mail in a manuscript with an editor's advance blessing is that he or she now feels at least a certain obligation to buy the thing. You've gone to a lot of work in the editor's behalf, at his request, and he knows it. If he now turns it down without an excellent reason (namely, you did a lousy job), you can be certain he'll feel a modicum of guilt.

Finally, the query letter protects your idea and should prevent the editor from giving the same or a similar assignment to some other freelancer. It's not unusual for several writers to submit almost identical story suggestions within the space of a few weeks. If your idea shows up first and the editor gives you a tentative go-ahead, ethics demand that he wait to review your effort before assigning the piece to someone else. With this in mind, you should submit your finished article as soon as practicable after receiving confirmation of editorial interest. And *never* accept such an assignment—even on speculation—without following through and mailing a manuscript. If an editor gives you the green light on an idea you've suggested, and the proposed article fails to turn up on his desk in a reasonable amount of time (two months at most, although two weeks is much better), you'll have a tough time getting serious consideration from that man in the future. If substantial research or extensive interviewing will be required before you can finish the article, more time may be needed. If this is the case, be sure you notify the editor of this at the time the assignment is made. Work out a suitable time frame that you both agree on, and then see that you meet the deadline.

Most full-time professionals won't sit down at the typewriter without an advance commitment from an editor, so by querying you automatically align yourself on the side of professionalism. And the more professional your approach, the more likely the editor is to take you seriously.

What makes an effective query letter? A good query should be short—never more than a single page—and to the point. You should tell the editor what you propose to write and why, while at the same time providing the human-interest angle. The query should excite his imagination and make him hungry to see the finished article. It should raise provocative questions—and promise to answer them. A query letter is nothing more than your sales pitch, and you should try to capture the editor's interest right from the beginning. Often, the lead sentence of your query letter can become the lead sentence of the article itself, since the same kind of hook is needed to compel the reader to keep reading. A catchy title is a big help, too.

Some beginning writers make the mistake of quickly dashing out a query letter just to get it in the mail. Since the query is in some ways more important than the article itself, the smart freelancer crafts this sales letter with all the professional care he can muster. If the query fails, the article dies aborning. Time spent drafting a really good query is an excellent investment. If the editor isn't already familiar with your work, the only way he has of judging your writing ability is through your query letter. If it exhibits a professional, lively style, he'll be more likely to gamble on your ability to produce a professional manuscript. On the other hand, if it's ungrammatical and contains strikeovers and spelling errors, you can be sure of being turned down. A dull, uninteresting query will meet with the same fate.

In the query letter, you should do your best to capture the editor's interest as soon as possible. Tell him why the article you're suggesting is unique, and why you think readers will find it useful, entertaining, or otherwise worthwhile. Let him know why you're qualified to write that particular piece—if you're an expert on the subject, tell him. On the other hand, don't feel obligated to advertise lack of expertise. It's always a mistake to announce that you're a beginner. You don't need to lie about past literary accomplishments—simply steer clear of the subject.

Incidentally, the query letter should always be addressed to the person listed on the masthead as editor or editor-in-chief. Sending queries to assistant editors, associate editors, or managing editors merely delays things, as the top editor generally is the only one who can make the final decision on assignments. Simply addressing correspondence to "editor" risks generating the same kind of enthusiasm on the part of the recipient as mail addressed "occupant." It certainly indicates you're not too familiar with the magazine. Use names—properly spelled—whenever possible.

If you're serious about becoming a freelancer, you might consider spending a few dollars to have a professional-looking letterhead drawn up and printed on your stationery. Most editors won't admit it, but I suspect this kind of touch gives you at least a slight edge over writers too tight to make this investment. In effect, your stationery serves as a professional calling card (you can have those printed, too) and helps camouflage any insecurities you feel as a beginner.

Like a manuscript, your query should have a logical beginning, middle, and end. While each letter needn't follow the same sequence, your first sentence should probably serve either as an interest-riveting hook or a straightforward announcement of what you want to write about. Again, an eye-catching title can help sell your idea, so try to work this in early, if possible.

The next paragraph should provide whatever backup information you need to convince the editor to buy. This covers everything from startling statistics that support your premise to particularly appealing quotes that spark human interest. This is also the place to list your own qualifications.

If you intend to provide photos or other graphic support, this point should be made, along with estimated length and delivery time. The final paragraph should close with your formal request for the assignment.

That's all the information you need to provide. Don't write at length in an attempt to bombard the editor with enough facts and figures to overwhelm her. Editors read a lot of manuscripts and proposals every day, and greatly appreciate brevity. If your query can't be presented in three, or maybe four, short paragraphs, you'd better do some more thinking on the subject. The theme may be too broad to be the subject of an effective article—or more likely, you merely need to simplify your presentation.

It should go without saying that your query letter—like your manuscript—should be neatly typed on good-quality paper. Most writers like twenty-pound bond with a high rag content. It's a temptation to submit on erasable bond, but editors hate the stuff because the shiny finish reflects light and makes the typing hard to read. It also tends to smudge easily. Even if your calligraphy is sufficiently beautiful to make John Hancock burn with envy, don't even think about inflicting it on a busy editor. If your submissions aren't typed—and that includes query letters—they won't be bought. It's that simple. If you don't know how to type and you hope to be a writer, you'd better start learning right now. In the meantime, it's always possible to hire someone to transform your scribblings into typed manuscript or letter form.

Some beginning writers succumb to the temptation to telephone an editor instead of writing him for an assignment.

There are times when such action is justified, but only on very rare occasions. If you have a fast-breaking story that must be acted on in too short a time to allow a written response, you might be forced to use the telephone. Editors tend to work under tight, sometimes frenetic schedules, and they most definitely do not appreciate telephoned interruptions. One of the surest ways to alienate an editor is to pester him with phone calls, particularly if you're a rank beginner with no established track record at that publication. Most such calls do a writer more harm than good when he's just starting out, so do your querying through the mail. Granted, it takes longer to get a response that way, but that written response has a much better chance of being favorable.

I've mentioned photo illustrations, but have yet to place the kind of stress on these graphics that they deserve. The vast majority of magazines published these days rely heavily on photographs to help put their message across, and most articles use at least some kind of illustration. I can't think of very many kinds of nonfiction submissions that wouldn't be greatly enhanced by good photo support, and many magazines won't even consider manuscripts that arrive without a selection of color slides or black-and-white prints.

I know many editors who will take the time to salvage a poorly written manuscript by extensive rewriting simply because it was accompanied by excellent photographs. At the beginner's level, good photos are much rarer than good writing, and the kind of graphic support made available with the piece often determines its final fate.

What kinds of photos will a magazine use? Study its published illustrations with the same care you use in dissecting the text. If you're handy with a camera, you can probably take the necessary pics yourself. A good 35mm camera is the best bet for this job. Even if you're not an experienced photographer, you can easily learn the basics of good picture-taking in a weekend.

If you doubt your ability with a camera, you may be able to make some kind of fee-splitting arrangement with a local professional photographer. I had such an arrangement when I began serious freelancing, and it worked out very well. Most magazines buy the manuscript and photos as a single package, and issue one check to cover both. I took 60 percent and my photographer got 40 percent. I know for a fact that having professional quality photographs to illustrate my articles helped them sell, and my photographer friend certainly earned his 40 percent of the resulting paychecks.

However, taking your own photographs isn't really all that difficult. I've been my own photographer for many years now, and I'm convinced that anyone smart enough to write salable copy can easily learn to take adequate photos. Every new camera comes with a set of instructions, and there are numerous pamphlets and books to help the beginner get started. Kodak offers several easy-to-follow photo booklets, and these are available in most camera stores. A visit to your local library should put literally dozens of other how-to photo books at your disposal. One factor separating the tyro from the pro is the professional's willingness to expend film. Shooting extra frames of each subject, using a slightly different exposure each time, is cheap insurance when you consider what it would cost you in time and money to go back and reshoot the whole thing.

When you're taking photos to support a planned article, remember that magazines that use color illustrations accept color slides only—not color prints. So buy the right kind of film—Kodachrome, Ektachrome, Fujichrome, or some other film that stipulates "for color slides" on the box. You can get acceptable black-and-white prints from almost any of the popular black-and-white films, but most pros use either Kodak Plus-X or Tri-X. Tri-X is faster, letting you shoot with less available light, but Plus-X has less objectionable grain. When submitting color, number the slides and protect them in one of the page-sized plastic sleeves that hold twenty 35mm slides. The caption material—information fully identifying what's happening in each picture—can be typed on a separate sheet with numbers to match. Most magazines that use black-and-white illustrations prefer 8-by-10-inch glossy prints. Be sure to send a good selection to give the art editor several choices. A dozen black-and-white prints may be enough, or a sleeve of twenty slides, although some magazines want more.

Photos sent through the mail should be protected by placing them against a sheet of cardboard or fiberboard and using rubber bands to bind the package together.

When you submit the manuscript itself, there's a more or less standard format every professional writer follows. Standard 8½-by-11-inch paper is used, with good twenty-pound bond the best choice. Generous margins give editors room to scribble the various proof marks needed to guide the typesetters as they work from the manuscript, and also leave a bit of space for minor changes to be penciled in. A left-hand margin of 1½ inches is about right, with a minimum of 1 inch of space left on the right-hand side of the page. Try to leave 1 or 1½ inches at the bottom.

On the first page of your manuscript, your name and address should appear, single-spaced, near the top at the left margin. Directly across on the right side of the page, you can indicate the type of rights you want to sell (normally "First North American Rights," although some magazines insist on purchasing "All Rights").

Everything else in the manuscript should be double-spaced. The title should appear centered on the page, about halfway down from the top. I use all capital letters for the title, although this isn't mandatory. Double space down from the title and center your byline: "by Jerald Q. Freelancer." Finally, drop down an additional two or three spaces and begin your first paragraph.

On succeeding pages, the manuscript title, your last name, and the page number should appear in the upper left corner: "Raising Tropical Ants/Freelancer/page 2." The text should continue a few spaces down.

All manuscripts should be mailed flat in manila envelopes sized large enough to accommodate the typewritten pages and accompanying photo illustrations. The pages should be paper-clipped—never stapled—together, and the whole works held together with rubber bands before being slipped into the envelope. A second envelope, folded in half if necessary, should be enclosed with the manuscript. This envelope should be addressed to yourself, and carry sufficient postage to insure the return of text and photos in case the editor declines to buy. Without a self-addressed return envelope, you will probably not get the package back if rejected.

While there are special postage rates available for manuscript copy, you're far better off paying first-class rates for the better service. Make sure the envelope is clearly marked "First Class" on both sides to make sure it doesn't travel third class by mistake. Allow at least four days for the manuscript to arrive, particularly when mailing coast-to-coast.

There's no need to send a lengthy cover letter along with your manuscript, as the work should be self-explanatory to any editor. In fact, the only legitimate reason to send a cover letter at all is to flag your article as one done on assignment (or at least with the editor's advance knowledge and consent) and not an over-the-transom submission. This gets your manuscript safely past the slush pile and directly to the editor's desk.

If you'll follow these guidelines and submit a neatly typed, grammatically correct, and properly spelled manuscript, that alone will go a long way toward insuring that your article gets serious consideration. A professionally prepared package stands out, and is something all editors are constantly on the lookout for.

If, in addition, you've carefully studied the magazine to determine the type of material it uses and needs, you'll be that much closer to a sale. If you've then followed up by writing an interesting, informative piece that tops the competition—and have provided suitable graphics for it—the sale is almost a sure thing.

Finally, don't become discouraged if you do collect a few rejection slips before you sell that first manuscript. Freelancing is a career that demands perseverance. Every writer has a collection of rejection slips tucked away in his or her files, and it's a fact that these disappointing bits of paper tend to be more numerous at the beginning of a freelancing career. As you learn your trade, rejections will become increasingly rare.

Building Repeat Sales

         Once an editor buys an article from you, you should see to it she doesn't subsequently forget your name. That first purchase gives you a foot in the door at that publishing house, and you should do your best to keep the door open.

If you've pleased an editor once, chances are excellent you can please her again. You know it, and the editor knows it—therefore, she should be less resistant to subsequent queries bearing your signature. You've proved your worth once, and you're missing a bet if you don't try to prove it time and time again.

A good writer-editor relationship is one of the most valuable things a freelancer can have. Once it gets started, it's up to you as a writer to nurture it along. This means doing all you can to keep that editor happy—and that, in turn, means keeping her steadily supplied with article ideas and well-written manuscripts.

Once you've managed to sell several pieces to an editor, she may begin counting on your output. These overworked administrators look long and hard for talent that pleases them, and when they find it they're almost as ecstatic as the fortunate freelancer. Nearly every editor has a stable of trusted writers she comes to rely on, and this small coterie of regular contributors may garner more than 80 percent of the assignments the magazine doles out.

As a side benefit, these regulars are the ones called for editor-generated assignments. Many of the ideas for interesting articles you see published each year originate with the magazine's editorial staff. Some of these articles end up being staff-written, but many are farmed out to freelancers. When the editor is calling you to make assignments, you'll be well past the submitting-on-speculation stage. After only a few successive sales to the same publication, agreed-on assignments should become just that—assignments. As long as you keep producing top-quality material, the words "on speculation" should no longer be part in your vocabulary when you talk with that particular editor.

How do you find yourself in this fortunate state of affairs? The answer is easy—simply be consistent in your work, and never let the editor down. If you acquire a reputation for turning out professional-quality manuscripts each and every time you complete an assignment, you'll be well on your way toward earning favored status.

However, writing consistently good copy is only half the battle. The photos you turn in must also be sharp and clear, and should show a degree of imagination. Give the magazine's art director a good selection of both vertically and horizontally oriented pictures to choose from. This gives him some leeway in making up a layout, and he'll love you for it. Try to make a few of the photos artfully posed or action-oriented, and be sure to include a couple of dramatic pics to be used as lead illustrations. By the time you've sold several articles to the magazine, you should have a pretty fair idea of the kinds of illustrations the publication prefers.

Punctuality can be even more important than finely honed prose or gallery-quality photographs when the editor is relying on you to meet a deadline. When you finally win your spurs as a trusted regular, the editor will begin depending more and more on your ability to turn your work in on time. He'll be planning issues with your upcoming article firmly scheduled in the table of contents, and if your contribution fails to show up when he needs it he'll be left with a big hole in his layout. If this happens, you're in trouble. Editors always have ways of filling such holes at the last minute, but it causes extra work and worry on their part—and they're harassed enough without your adding to their problems. The first time this happens, you may be let off with a simple Scotch blessing—*provided* you have an excellent excuse for your tardiness. This had better be on the order of a death in the family (your pet cat doesn't count), serious illness, or an auto accident injury. Be warned in advance that any editor who's been in the business long enough to have his name on the masthead has already heard every explanation in the book. If your excuse doesn't fit one of the above three categories, don't try to come up with something less plausible. Your editor won't be impressed. If a delay appears unavoidable for some reason that's out of your immediate control, don't wait until the last minute to let the editor find out. Give him a call and advise him that your manuscript may be late. If he knows about it early enough, no sweat—he'll be able to schedule some other article to fill the hole. It's those last-minute surprises that turn him off to a contributor.

If you send your copy in late a second time, you've substantially lowered your stock with that editor. Magazines are typeset, dummied, printed, and bound on tight schedules, and shipping deadlines have to be met. Manuscripts turned in on time or a few days early help the editorial staff keep work flowing smoothly. Tardy assignments foul things up, and no editor will put up with a writer who can't be depended on to meet stipulated deadlines. As a practical matter, most editors assign due dates with a few days of "fat" built into the schedule, simply to insure that they have all the necessary copy at hand when it's time to start working on the next issue. This means you can sometimes shave an assigned deadline a little close without getting burnt, but don't count on it. If it looks like you're going to have trouble meeting the editor's timetable, be sure to let him know about it as soon as possible. Your key to receiving assignments on anything approaching a regular basis is the record of proven dependability you've earned with that publication. Guard it at all costs.

Eventually, you may become well enough known by an editor to call him on the telephone once in a while. He may even tell you to call him or may leave messages requesting return calls. In fact, it's possible to reach the point in an editorial relationship where the majority of correspondence between writer and editor is conducted over the telephone. Such an arrangement has several advantages from the freelancer's point of view.

In the first place, there's no built-in time lag between query and reply. You get a yes or no to suggested ideas immediately, and this can free you to submit the idea elsewhere right away. Even more important, you've established two-way communication that allows a free exchange of ideas and opinions. If the editor has some objection to an article you've proposed, you may be able to make a counterproposal that eliminates the stumbling block. Very often I've found that such conversations result in multiple assignments, simply because you usually end up discussing a variety of subjects before you hang up the phone.

If an editor is expecting your call, and if you've planned what you want to say well enough to keep the conversation short and to the point, telephoned queries can save both parties time. If the editor can give an instant reply to your queries and make assignments on the spot, he won't need to dictate a written answer later. However, if your call catches the editor in conference or at some important task he hates to break away from, it may not be well received. Telephone calls are often viewed as unwelcome interruptions in a busy work schedule, and the writer who makes a pest of himself with too-frequent calls is only hurting his chances. Too, some editors hate to be pressured by the need to make an instant decision. They may prefer to think things over thoroughly before offering a firm commitment, and sometimes regret assignments made on the spur of the moment.

In other words, the telephone is an instrument to be used with discretion, if at all, in your dealings with editors. The beginning writer should *never* call to ask for an assignment, and even experienced pros should exercise extreme circumspection in their telephone contacts. It's usually a good idea to wait for the editor to initiate a telephone relationship. Once she's called you a few times, she certainly shouldn't object if you return the favor. Even so, it's advisable to come to some kind of understanding about phone calls very early in this type of exchange. Simply ask the editor if she'd mind your calling her when you have a particularly hot idea to discuss. If she gives you the go-ahead, make sure you don't abuse the privilege.

There's one kind of phone call that should almost never be made—at least if you hope to continue selling to that editor on a regular basis. I'm referring to anxious calls made to check on the status of a manuscript that was mailed last month. If you don't hear from a magazine about the fate of your submission after a reasonable period of time—say six or eight weeks—it's accepted practice to send a polite note inquiring into its status. Simply ask if the article has been received, and briefly request a status report. But whatever you do, *mail* this request. Don't use the telephone to seek such information! The only time you should even consider calling an editor about such a subject would be after at least two of your letters—spaced a month or more apart—have been successively ignored. Then a phone call is in order. But first give the editor a chance to reply to your written queries.

Dunning an editor over the long-distance wires is another excellent way to alienate yourself from future assignments. Such tactics sometimes become necessary, as some magazines are slow to pay their contributors. When a check you have coming is long overdue, the polite course is to send a courteous reminder that you have yet to be paid. If this doesn't do the trick, you're justified in making a call. I'll discuss this kind of unfortunate action further in chapter 6. The point I want to make here is that harrassing phone calls—even if they're justified—can quickly cut you off from future consideration by the editor involved.

Once you reach the point in your writing career that you're selling regularly to a few editors, it's a good idea to try to meet them in person. Most magazine publishers are located in New York City or on the West Coast, and this may be off the beaten path for a freelancer living in Denver or Des Moines. However, it's well worth a writer's time to schedule side trips that will bring her to an editor's desk if vacations are planned anywhere near the magazine's editorial offices. Having a face and a personality to match up with those query letters or phone calls makes a big difference to an editor, whether he'll admit it or not. Every businessman knows that the personal touch brings big dividends, and that's what freelancers basically are—businessmen. I know several well-known writers living in the West who fly to New York at least once a year just to renew those valuable relationships face to face. Such an excursion costs several hundred dollars, but the serious professional views this as a necessary business expense. I know from experience that such tactics pay off. Once you get to know an editor and meet with him personally, your sales to that magazine can escalate dramatically.

A word of caution here—don't hound an editor for a personal appointment if you haven't sold him several pieces in the recent past. Editors are extremely busy people, and if they don't get their work done before the five o'clock whistle blows they simply have to stay chained to their desks until they get caught up. I've never met an editor who was able to observe the traditional forty-hour workweek; most put much more time on the clock, usually without extra pay. So if you waste fifteen minutes or a half hour of their time, they're the ones who suffer for it later. For this reason, editors aren't anxious to meet writers they're not already fairly well acquainted with through past correspondence and assignments. They've got better things to do than shake the hand of every would-be writer who happens to be passing through the neighborhood. Even if you have a burning desire to write for his magazine and are supplied with a briefcase full of surefire ideas to discuss, he won't want to see you. The initial contact should always be made through a well-thought-out query letter or by simply sending a manuscript along for the editor's consideration.

On the other hand, a regular contributor can almost always be assured of a warm welcome. That editor is probably as anxious to meet you as you are to see him, and if he has any extra time at all in his schedule you'll be welcome to it. However, you may catch him at a bad time—editors have to attend numerous planning meetings, and on shipping day (when all the page layouts go to the printer), these busy men and women are at their most harried. So it's best to write or call in advance for at least a tentative appointment. And if the editor is otherwise occupied at the moment you arrive, be patient until he can see you. When you're finally ushered in, don't try to monopolize his time for the next hour or so. Be considerate and keep the meeting short. Ten minutes of conversation are all you really need to accomplish your purpose, although some editors may spend a half hour or more with you if they have the time and interest. To use this time to best advantage, it's a good idea to have one or two new article ideas well developed and ready to present. You may not leave with an assignment, but at least the editor won't feel you've wasted his time.

Many specialized magazines are highly product-oriented, and their editors make it a practice to attend one or more trade shows each year to stay abreast of new developments in the field. If you contribute regularly to such a magazine, it can be well worth your while to visit the same show. This offers you yet another opportunity to meet with the editor, and he'll usually be able to spend more time with you than he would at the office. Such a trip is almost guaranteed to pay for itself many times over in extra assignments, and if you take a few hours to check out manufacturers' display booths before your meeting, chances are you'll be able to garner several new assignments on the spot. Again, it's always a good idea to check with the editor in advance to make sure he'll actually be attending the show, and to set up a definite appointment.

When you show this kind of initiative, an editor can't help but be impressed. He knows you're shelling out hard-earned cash when you have to travel halfway across the country to take in a trade show. He also knows that this action will benefit him, and that you hope it will be of benefit to you, as well. Obviously, you can't afford to spend four hundred or five hundred dollars on airplane fares and hotel bills if there isn't a good prospect of realizing an even greater return. This is something only you can be the judge of. Again, this is a subject we'll cover more thoroughly in chapter 6.

When you have an editor buying from you regularly, that isn't the time to slack off and turn your best attempts toward selling to another publication. You can't sit on past laurels. If the quality of your work starts to slip or shows less imagination, you can easily find yourself on the sidelines again. I'm not advising you to limit your contributions to one or two magazines. But I am encouraging you to expend more—not less—effort when an editor likes your work and shows it by making you a regular contributor.

That's the time to redouble your efforts and show that editor how valuable you really are. Use your imagination to develop new approaches to favorite subjects, or to come up with exciting lead stories that could boost newsstand sales. Try to make your work stand out. Only by receiving regular assignments is it possible to build anything approaching a steady income from freelancing, and if you can convince an editor that he needs something from you each month, your cash flow will achieve a certain happy stability.

While turning out accurate, readable copy on time will go a long way toward cementing your long-term relationship with an editor, there are some definite no-no's to avoid. For instance, you should never sell a too-similar article to a competing publication—at least not in the same two-year time span. If you have two articles about widgets appearing in separate publications with only a few months' time lapse, the editors of both magazines may become justifiably upset. The pieces may not be identical—and you'd better hope they're not unless you're ready to become involved in a publisher's lawsuit—but editors hope for at least a degree of exclusivity when they purchase a manuscript. The only possible exception might be if the two magazines in question were in no way competitive—in other words, of entirely different types, and with widely differing readerships. If you can sell a piece about widgets to both the *Ladies' Home Journal* and *The American Rifleman*, go to it! As long as the treatment isn't identical, neither of these editors would be likely to object.

Some writers try to get extra mileage from their work by peddling a spin-off piece under a pseudonym. Again, this can be a respectable practice as long as the purchasers aren't too competitive. However, it doesn't take long for these kinds of shenanigans to catch up with you if you stay in the same editorial neighborhood.

An editor you're selling to regularly may suggest using two or more of your articles in the same issue, with the understanding that a pseudonym will be used on at least one of the pieces. Editors do this to hide the fact that the same writer's work is appearing so often. Some freelancers object to this, as they feel that having their own name in print is too valuable to their careers to allow it to be replaced with an alias. Refusing to use a pseudonym when requested can only cost you money, and the editor isn't likely to suggest such multiple coverage a second time. My own work has appeared under several different pen names, and the resulting checks cashed just as satisfactorily as when Clair Rees got the published credit. Most professional, financially solvent writers will advise you not to let ego stand in the way of income.

A writer-editor relationship should be one of mutual trust. The time may come when you'll feel justified in "firing" an editor—some people in publishing simply can't bring themselves to treat writers fairly, while others aren't allowed to—but you should never find yourself with the roles reversed. If you work conscientiously and do your best to please the editor who favors you with regular assignments, you should be able to hold up your end of the relationship.

Turn in top-quality text and photos, and always try to write with an entertaining flair. Submit your articles on time, and make sure all your facts are accurate. Present clean, readable packages, and keep your editor well supplied with fresh, well-thought-out ideas for future assignments. If you must use the telephone, don't overdo it—and never call repeatedly without the editor's prior consent.

The trick to garnering regular repeat assignments is to make yourself—or rather, your contributions—indispensable to an editor. Once she comes to rely on you to help her put her magazine together, your earnings will start to climb. Since those second, third, and fourth assignments come easier than the first one, it only makes good sense to concentrate your early efforts on editors who have proven to be receptive in the past.

Versatility vs. Specialization

One of the decisions a freelancer must face early in his career is whether to specialize and build up his name in a particular field, or take a shotgun approach in marketing his work. Both tactics offer certain advantages to the writer, and both have their share of drawbacks.

Writing for several entirely different markets helps keep a freelancer from going stale, and can become an education in itself. You learn something new with almost every assignment, and develop versatility. What's more, working for a broad spectrum of publishers helps spread risk. Some writing fields are so narrowly defined that the entire market comprises one or two magazines. Obviously, it wouldn't be wise to select such a limited specialty—in the first place, these extremely technical magazines don't usually pay enough to keep even a part-time freelancer in more than pocket change. Besides, if even one of these magazines goes out of business, there's not much left of your market.

Spreading your work around among different types of publishers gives you the chance to determine which fields you feel most comfortable in. Some freelancers find that they enjoy interviewing and writing about people, while others are temperamentally better suited to sports or travel stories. Still others become mechanically oriented and collect their magazine income with "how-to-build-it" articles or product reviews. While the magazine fiction market offers nowhere near the opportunities it did a decade ago, there are writers who continue to eke out livings from nothing more than their typewriters and vivid imaginations.

Most experienced professionals are versatile enough to write authoritatively for widely varied publications, and many do. Some use a different pseudonym for each market, reasoning that readers wouldn't readily accept a gourmet cook equally skilled in river-running or business finance. Others adopt pen names to disguise their sex—readers of women's magazines may insist on a woman's point of view, while some male-oriented periodicals are equally chauvinistic.

Another advantage of becoming diversified is that you don't become trapped in a constricted market. It's possible for a writer's name to become overexposed in a field where only three or four different magazines are being published. If her byline appears once or twice in every related publication on the newsstands, editors may become wary of this prolificacy. At the same time, no one magazine may be able to offer rates high enough to allow the freelancer the luxury of working on an exclusive basis.

The beginning writer may be well advised to concentrate on a single market, at least at the start. Specialization is the key to rapid repeat sales, and is one way to quickly develop a reputation for professional expertise. Editors keep a keen eye on the competition, and once your byline appears a few times in one publication, you'll have little difficulty selling to similar magazines. If you do a good job and turn in clean, competent copy, you can create a mildly competitive situation. In spite of what you might hear in college creative writing courses, and the huge number of unsolicited manuscripts received by magazines to the contrary, there is a real shortage of professional talent available to editors in many semispecialized fields. When a new writer who proves to be both capable and dependable surfaces, he is quickly made welcome.

In the previous chapter I pointed out that once you make a sale to an editor, there is increasingly less resistance on her part to future sales. Editors are always happy to find talent that pleases them, and it's only natural for them to be more receptive to queries and manuscripts from a writer of proven worth than they are likely to be toward the efforts of still another unknown. Thus, specialization may actually be thrust upon you as you follow the course of least resistance. It only makes good business sense to take advantage of an editor's inclination to favor her magazine's writing alumni in doling out monthly assignments, and before you know it you may be enjoying staff status on the masthead. Being listed as a contributing editor or part of a magazine's staff may not bring you a regular monthly salary, but it's a sign that you're well established with that publication and probably contributing on a monthly or bimonthly basis. It also gives you a tiny bit of extra professional prestige, and looks good on a résumé the next time you change jobs. (There can be a danger in listing such after-hours accomplishments on employment forms if you're a part-time freelancer holding a regular job. This is discussed in detail in chapter 7.)

If you become particularly well known for your writing in a certain specialty area, you're likely to achieve "expert" status in the eyes of editors. This can lead to assignments or even regular columns in more general magazines with related interests. Some writers who gained an early reputation as automotive experts while writing for tightly specialized car, truck, and four-wheel-drive magazines have gone on to more lucrative assignments in the better-paying outdoor sport or men's magazines. While automotive writing itself is a narrowly defined specialty, there are a number of high-circulation publications that can and do use automotive-related material every now and then. Some magazines with a largely male readership schedule automotive features regularly, while others run a monthly column on the subject.

The same holds true for other writing specialties. There are many instances where freelancers who have earned expert status working for special-interest publications have later caught the eye of a mass-market magazine editor.

As a matter of fact, there are a number of well-known writers who had no intention of becoming professional freelancers when they started out. Many of these people simply had an area of expertise they felt could profitably be shared with others, and took a shot at writing about it. Some didn't even take the initiative this far, but were pushed under protest to the typewriter by some friend or editor who thought their specialized knowledge would make interesting reading.

There are so many successful writers who wandered in from other fields—engineering, data processing, teaching, law enforcement, you name it—that I suspect the majority of selling freelancers have never had formal writing training. At least there are relatively few who were exposed to anything more rigorous, as far as writing was concerned, than freshman English composition. A graduate degree in English or journalism certainly isn't a prerequisite to writing success.

Once these "nonwriter" freelancers overcome their initial shyness about putting words on paper, they often discover they actually enjoy the task. After being published repeatedly in the specialty magazines that got them started in the trade, they may gain sufficient confidence in their authorship abilities to try writing outside their area of recognized expertise. If they're again successful, yet another freelancing career is launched.

That some writers enter the profession through this apparently unlikely back door illustrates the value of specializing early. Becoming recognized as an authority in a particular writing field can give you the springboard you'll need to diversify later on.

While specialization may be good advice for the beginning freelancer who wants to build a name for herself in a hurry, there are pitfalls to watch out for. Some writers become so comfortable in their chosen specialty that they're never tempted to try other fields. That's not always bad, however. Some specialized writers become so well known and successful at what they do that there's little incentive for them to test the water in other ponds. A writer earning top dollar writing about a certain subject may have difficulty justifying time spent building a reputation in a field where she's still unknown. Once you become accustomed to a comfortable level of recompense for your freelancing efforts, simple economics may force you to remain in your specialty. If you can earn $1000 for an article about a subject on which you're a recognized authority, it doesn't make sense to spend the same amount of time—or even more—writing another kind of piece commanding one-tenth the fee. To top the matter off, the better-paying assignment will probably be just that—a definite assignment, with a firm commitment on the part of the editor to purchase it. The nickel-and-dime effort is apt to be speculative, as your reputation may not be transferable to unrelated periodicals.

Some editors won't allow themselves to be impressed with your success in other publishing areas, reasoning that a history of writing science-oriented articles for *Mechanics Illustrated* or *Popular Science* may not be the ideal qualification for the celebrity interviews *People* magazine wants. The fact that you've demonstrated professional writing skills in your work for other magazines will probably give you an edge over the rank beginners you'll be competing with, but this may not count for much. When you start writing in a field completely unrelated to the one you've been working in, essentially you're starting over. You have to prove your worth all over again, and that means taking lower pay than you're used to until your new reputation is solidly established.

For the full-time freelancer who must earn top dollar for his time, this prospect isn't very attractive. He has only so much writing time available each day, and this time must be put to the best possible use—that means receiving adequate pay for his effort. If he must average $200 a day, he can't accept too many $100 assignments unless they're short pieces he can toss off between breakfast and lunch.

One answer to this is to branch out gradually. Expand your efforts into related fields instead of striking out in entirely new directions, and you should be able to take better advantage of your hard-won reputation. For instance, I know of a writer who got his start composing articles for firearms magazines. These magazines are narrowly specialized, and while some pay fairly well the overall rate schedule is low. As a result, the freelance competition is similarly low-keyed.

After publishing a number of firearms pieces, the writer earned a small reputation in this specialized field. He then turned to the larger hunting and fishing magazines, where his past reputation gained him fast entry. He first wrote about hunting, which was a logical extension of his firearms experience, and then turned his attention to fishing and camping pieces. Since the large-circulation general outdoor magazines also publish these kinds of articles, the editorial acceptance he had achieved with his hunting tales made it easy for him to sell the other manuscripts. He further broadened his area of expertise by evaluating and reviewing binoculars, tents, backpacking gear, and other outdoor equipment. He wrote some humorous outdoor articles, and then began writing similar material for airline in-flight magazines and other general-interest publications.

He stretched his outdoor writing base further to encompass pickup trucks and four-wheel-drive vehicles, and parlayed this experience into mechanically oriented pieces for the science and mechanics market. Outdoor cooking skills were likewise diverted to other large-circulation magazines as this writer expanded his marketability one logical step at a time.

This is an approach that makes a lot of sense—specialize until you've built up a receptive market among one group of editors, then expand that specialty to closely related fields and write for an increasing number of magazines.

How do you parlay publishing success with small, specialized, low-paying magazines into a general writing career in more lucrative markets? Do as the gun writer did and look for large-circulation magazines with readers likely to have an interest in the subjects you've covered for specialty publications. You'll need to broaden your approach, but this isn't difficult. For instance, there are magazines devoted to serious bicyclists and hikers, and these publications tend to use technical or at least semitechnical material related to advances in equipment or techniques. Such a narrow focus wouldn't appeal to a general-interest magazine like *Family Circle* or *McCall's*, but a "Joys of Bicycling" for busy adults piece might find a home here. If you slanted your approach to play up the health and exercise aspect with a title like "Cycle Your Way Back to Size Seven," and sprinkled the manuscript with a few "calories used up per hour" figures and a quote or two from medical or diet experts to back up your premise, the idea should be salable to any woman's magazine.

Men worry about their waistlines, too, and by changing your focus slightly you could sell a similar piece to *Esquire*. Take a college-athlete approach or chronicle the latest in lightweight, luxury two-wheeler imports in a lively, sexy fashion, and *Playboy* may even be within reach.

Once you've sold your bicycling piece to any of these high-paying magazines, you have a foot in the door and the editor is likely to give serious consideration to other ideas you come up with. Thus, you gain an editorial audience for non-bicycling articles. Since you've by now earned a small reputation as an exercise writing expert, you might suggest a piece on isometrics or some other muscle-toning activity that can be performed while viewing television at home. Or you could take another tack and quote medical opinions on the *dangers* of jogging. Thus you can continually broaden your writing background.

Gaining a writing reputation in any particular market takes time, but as your byline appears with increasing frequency, assignments become easier to get and editors will start seeking you out. What's more, your fees should go up as you become better known.

It's possible to earn expert standing in two or three widely differing fields simultaneously, and many writers do this. However, directing your energies along several different paths dilutes their force, and can lengthen the time it takes to achieve recognition in any of the chosen markets.

Should you specialize or try for the diversified approach? If you're a beginning freelancer, the answer will depend on your immediate and long-term goals. If you intend to pursue freelance writing simply as a more or less lucrative hobby, you can start either way. The challenge of communicating with different interest groups can be exciting and rewarding, and adding a varied list of magazines to your publishing credits can be highly ego-satisfying. It should also help establish your reputation as a versatile writer, and may aid your regular nine-to-five career.

However, I've already pointed out that early specialization is a proven path to accelerated sales. If you're hungry for fast—if limited—recognition and firm assignments in place of "on speculation" go-aheads, this may be the best route to follow. From a commercial, dollars-and-cents point of view, confining your energy to a particular market area does have its advantages. At least this is true for the beginning freelancer. Part-time writers have but a limited amount of time to devote to their publishing careers, and one of the best ways to hurry that career along is to channel those efforts into a single area. This is also an excellent way to gain the kind of credibility a beginning book author needs. When you establish a reputation in any particular area of writing expertise, book publishers are likely to pay more attention to your nonfiction proposal about that specialty than they would to a sales pitch from someone with less verifiable experience.

While specialization is one method of getting your freelancing career off to a fast start, you won't want to limit yourself too narrowly once it's well under way. This is particularly true if you hope to turn to freelancing on a full-time basis. While there are some writing specialties that can become lucrative enough to support a growing family in at least marginal style, the opportunities are few and far between. If you manage to land a regular salaried position as a contributing editor of a publication, or are able to write a book or two each year to supplement your magazine-writing income, you may be able to stay afloat financially without venturing too far from familiar subject matter. This means reaching a level of security few highly specialized writers ever achieve. That's not to say it can't be done, but you're bucking some heavy odds.

Furthermore, there's always a young, hungry writer snapping at your heels, and you can't count on holding any editorial position forever. As a matter of fact, there is traditionally a pretty fast turnover among in-house editing staffs, and when a new editor-in-chief comes aboard there's often a re-rigging of the magazine's entire masthead. The competition is keen at the top in any business, and freelance writing is certainly no exception.

As a result, many full-time freelancers who are serious about keeping their families fed from the typewriter diversify. By pursuing other specialties and gradually earning recognition in three or four writing fields, they spread their employment risk. One of the big advantages of freelancing for a living stems from the lack of dependency on any single income source. If an editor becomes disenchanted with your work—or vice versa—it isn't too serious if a half-dozen other editors buy from you regularly. If you rely on a single magazine for the bulk of your income, you might just as well be punching a factory time clock. It's nice to have some kind of steady paycheck coming in, but most writers don't feel comfortable making all their money at a single source. If that source suddenly dries up, you're in deep trouble!

In addition to spreading risk, diversifying can help maximize your writing income. The more magazines you write for regularly, the larger your market. This in turn gives you greater income potential. However, you want to be earning the top dollar available in each market, and building this expertise isn't the kind of thing you do overnight.

Writing about different subject areas is a good way to keep from going stale. When you spend several years writing about a particular specialty, you may begin to repeat yourself. This can be disconcerting, and might induce a monumental case of writer's block. When you start worrying about original ways to say the same old things, it's probably time you started to develop some different markets.

You can get into a real rut if you write for a single, narrowly defined market year in and year out. The work that was once such a joy slowly turns to simple drudgery, and deadlines become harder and harder to meet. This is how most writing slumps start out, and some slumps last long enough to put a freelancer out of business.

The cure is to avoid limiting your creativity to a single area of expertise. Most people turn to writing as a profession because they enjoy it. When ideas seem fresh and new, the fun remains. But a professional freelancer must be surprisingly prolific to make a living at what she does, and some writers turn out between one hundred and two hundred magazine articles every year. Others restrict their output to a fraction of that, and market their work only to top-paying publications. But even this latter group turns out an awful lot of copy from month to month, and this can become tiring if the writer stays in the same general subject area.

There's a great deal of truth in the old saw, "a change is as good as a rest," and the ability to switch to a completely different type of writing assignment when another manuscript becomes boring is excellent stimulation.

Having more subject areas of potentially profitable interest should make you a better-rounded writer. The ability to turn out competent material on diverse topics is one test of the true professional, and all some freelancers ask is sufficient time to research the subject before tackling an unfamiliar assignment. These generalists aren't as common as they once were among practicing freelancers, but there are still many magazine contributors who cheerfully accept assignments requiring considerable study and preparation. The drawback here is the possibility that your research time will eat up all your profits—or at least bring your dollars-per-hour earnings down below the legal minimum-wage level. Miscalculating the preparation time an article will require is an occupational hazard all writers face, and chronic underestimation will drastically lower your income. This is one reason some writers prefer to stay within—or very close to—a chosen specialty. They're sufficiently knowledgeable about the subjects they're apt to be assigned to estimate almost exactly how much time they'll spend in preparation. Thus, they can accurately evaluate proffered fees before accepting the commission and can insure that their work on the piece will be sufficiently remunerative.

In short, both diversification and specialization have their advantages, and the path you should take depends on several different considerations. What are your goals as a freelancer? If you intend to write only as a part-time hobby and income isn't a major concern, you can query any magazine that strikes your fancy. You don't really need a game plan.

If, on the other hand, you hope to achieve rapid recognition and enjoy expert status among a group of readers and editors, specialization is the way to go. This is an excellent way to avoid collecting too many early rejection slips. Once an editor finally buys, there's a good chance she'll be willing to become a repeat customer. Later on, you can use this writing base as a springboard to broader markets.

At the same time, specializing too long or too narrowly can take much of the fun out of writing and may eventually affect the quality of your work. Limiting your marketplace is also likely to limit your long-term earning potential. Diversification can help keep your syntax lively and readable, and serve as a safety hedge should your prime market dry up.

In the same way a careful stockbroker minimizes her client's financial risk by purchasing a variety of unrelated securities instead of investing all available funds in one place, a smart writer will hedge his bets by avoiding complete dependency on a single freelancing specialty. There are magazine writers who manage to make a respectable living from a particular type of magazine, so it can be done. However, most successful freelancers who do this invest some time in writing a book or two each year. If there's a large enough market to support this kind of output, you may not need more than one lone specialty.

Every writer has different financial and psychological needs, and these can be satisfied in various ways. I've done my best to explain the advantages and pitfalls of each path. In the final analysis, the decision to specialize or diversify your freelancing skills is yours alone.

The Business Side of Writing

Once you've learned what editors like and how to supply it, you should take a hard look at the income your efforts are bringing in. It's a sad reality that freelance writers as a group are some of the most underpaid people in the country. If you're serious about making money with your freelancing skills, you must make sure you don't remain a member of the underpaid majority.

While our artistic souls would prefer it otherwise, publishing is a business, pure and simple. Publishers and those who invest in publishing houses share a single common goal: They want to see their business make a profit. Not a marginal profit but a big one—the bigger the better. One long-traditional method of insuring profits from any business enterprise is to hold costs to a minimum. The manuscripts editors purchase from freelancers represent one regular cost-factor of publishing, and as dutiful employees these editors do their best to hold this expense down. If they don't do it, you can bet that their publishers will.

In simple terms, that means any editor you have dealings with will be trying to buy your product—your manuscripts and illustrations—as cheaply as possible. This isn't the editor's fault. Many editors were once freelancers themselves, and they sympathize with your plight. Unfortunately, that sympathy may not extend to the point that the editor is willing to incur the displeasure of her publisher boss by insisting that freelancers' fees be raised. If you doubt this, look at the rates magazines paid a decade ago, and compare these figures with today's pay schedules. The majority of magazines haven't increased their advertised pay rates more than marginally in the last ten years, and many haven't changed them at all. Considering the effect inflation has had on the dollar over the same time period, in terms of true buying power these publications are purchasing manuscripts for less than half what they once paid.

To compound this economic absurdity, some magazines have actually *reduced* their rates in recent years, and today pay substantially less for articles than they did back when a buck would buy three or four gallons of gas.

A look at the advertising rates these same publications charge shows a considerably different picture. Ad revenues have gone way up, while editorial purchasing budgets remain more or less constant. In other words, the freelancer is getting the short end of the stick. She has to run harder and harder even to stay in the same place financially, let alone get ahead.

How did this sad state of affairs come about? More importantly, how can periodicals continue to get away with this kind of parsimony? Are well-written articles actually worth less these days? Or are there arcane forces at work in the literary marketplace?

The fact is, the editorial market is like any other inasmuch as its prices reflect the age-old balance between supply and demand. Simply speaking, it's a buyer's market. For every writer who's selling regularly, a hundred others are clamoring to see their bylines in print. Inevitably, this keeps prices low, and there's the unspoken threat that if a writer becomes too insistent in his demands for better pay, the editor will simply drop him from the contributors' list and buy from someone else.

While this threat is in some respects real, it doesn't mean article rates aren't negotiable. Some writers acquire a reputation for turning in clean, professional copy, and proven performance is always worth more in this one-sided market. Extensive copyediting costs editorial time and wages, so it makes economic sense to pay some kind of premium for manuscripts requiring little editing before being sent to the typesetter.

Unfortunately, you can't count on your editor to pass this helpful information along. He may voluntarily increase your pay rate in time, but this may never happen unless you voice a complaint. In more than a dozen years of professional writing, I've enjoyed numerous and sometimes substantial raises in pay—but I can recall only three such increases offered without prodding on my part. The sad fact is, you may never get more money for your writing effort unless you ask for it. This is something some writers never build up enough nerve to do, and is yet another reason editorial pay rates remain so low. (More on this later on in the chapter.)

Paltry pay is but one of the economic problems facing the serious freelancer. Many magazines notoriously tight-fisted with their word rates add insult by paying only on—or sometimes well after—publication. It can be several months or even a year or more before the writer sees her money. In addition to depriving the freelance businessperson payment owed him for protracted periods of time, this pay-on-publication policy not infrequently results in cancellation of the project. Editorial plans change periodically, and editors themselves tend to play musical chairs as they move from magazine to magazine. The article one editor gave a firm go-ahead six months ago may not fit the tastes of his successor—or the original purchaser may simply change his mind. In either case, your "assigned" piece never sees print, and in place of the check you've been promised you'll get your manuscript back with a brief "sorry" note attached.

Magazines that follow this policy claim they simply can't afford to pay on acceptance, and don't have sufficient capital to maintain an editorial backlog representing three or four months' work. In other words, they want to operate on your money. They could just as easily obtain bank financing to underwrite their business, but banks charge interest. By refusing to pay the freelancer until after her work is published, the magazine essentially is getting an interest-free loan.

The injustice of this popular practice is twofold: First, the publisher is taking full advantage of the freelancer's insecurity—she wouldn't dare ask the printer, the typesetter, or her own in-house staff to wait for their money. They'd all walk off the job and put her out of business. Only the writer will stand still for this kind of foolishness. What hurts even more is that the money withheld from the freelancer's pocket represents but a tiny fraction of the publisher's costs. Charges for typesetting, printing, paper, postage, wages, office rental, and so on make up the bulk of expense incurred in producing and distributing a magazine; the editorial budget for buying manuscripts is insignificant in comparison. By withholding payment from freelance contributors, the publisher is saving what amounts to pin money.

Asking a freelancer to write an article for payment on publication is similar to asking a contractor to build you a house with the stipulation that you won't give him any money until you've moved into the completed home and lived in it for awhile—always remembering that you have the option of changing your mind at any time and canceling the project. In other words, you're asking the contractor-businessperson to invest considerable amounts of time and material in building a structure to your specifications, without any binding commitment on your part to buy.

After all, the builder can always sell his home to someone else, can't he? The fact that he may have trouble disposing of a house with five bathrooms on the main floor and the living room upstairs is hardly your concern.

Thus reasons the editor. If he doesn't actually *use* your manuscript, he's not obligated to do anything more than return it to you (assuming you remembered to supply a stamped, self-addressed mailing envelope when you submitted the piece). If his conscience really pricks, he might deign to send along a personal note of condolence, but don't count on it. And the best of British luck in selling your feature on parakeet pinfeathers elsewhere. Kill fees are one answer to this problem, and I'll talk about those in a minute.

"Low pay —slow pay" publications are the reason so many would-be freelancers go broke every year, and it would be nice if "pay on publication" magazines could be forced to change their ways. However, this isn't likely to happen in the foreseeable future—at least not as long as there are so many hungry writers out there willing—even eager—to put up with such treatment.

Like the majority of freelancers, I started out writing for POP ("pay on publication") magazines, and I must admit that most did their best to honor editorial commitments—not all, but most. While I didn't appreciate the policy, it was something I could live with while my groceries and rent came from another source. I was too eager to make the sale to question too closely the payment arrangements involved. In fact, I often didn't know exactly how much an editor was paying for a piece until the check arrived in the mail. I trusted editors to treat me fairly, and most of them did. I wasn't getting rich, but I was publishing. When a check did come, it would spark a mild celebration and we'd have steak for dinner.

The fact that there are so many freelancers who write on a part-time basis and have this very attitude toward payment is another reason full-time writers have such difficulty receiving fair treatment. Full-time professionals are a tiny minority compared to the hordes of part-timers and outright hobbyists they're competing with, and most magazines are geared to buying from the occasional writer. Thus, even respected magazines that do pay their contributors on acceptance may take several weeks—or even a few months—to get a check in the mail. It may take two or three weeks after an assignment arrives in house for the editor to get around to reading it, and then he generally mails the writer a contract (more about this in just a minute). Getting your signature on this agreement and transporting it back to the editor adds a built-in delay of a week or more, and only then does the editor submit a voucher to the accounting department. Depending on accounting's inflexible schedule (if the deadline for this week's business is missed, it may be another fortnight before your voucher receives further attention), it can take up to three weeks to issue a check. If the person who prints the checks is ill or on vacation, which apparently happens with surprising frequency at some publications, the process can take considerably longer. In other words, you can't expect to see a check in your mailbox three days after an article has been accepted, even when you're selling to a magazine that pays on acceptance. Some magazines do mail payments out promptly—one such jewel I've been contributing to regularly for several years is famous for getting cash into a freelancer's hand within two weeks of the time the manuscript hits the editor's desk. In contrast, other "name" publications require from one to three months to perform this task.

While there's not much a writer can do to speed payment from a giant publishing corporation that observes peculiarly time-consuming accounting rites, there are ways to win better treatment from "low pay—slow pay" markets.

If an editor likes your material enough to buy it regularly, he should be willing to make concessions regarding the amount and speed of payment. Normally, an editor pays a new writer a certain minimum rate. When the freelancer proves himself through subsequent sales, his work should be worth more than rock-bottom minimum. The problem here is that unless the writer *asks* for more money, there's no motivation for the editor to give it to him. As long as the contributor is willing to accept the low pay scale he started out with, the publisher is usually very happy to maintain the status quo.

Freelancers as a group are notoriously poor businessmen, and they're generally insecure about editor-writer relationships. They're reluctant to offend editors kind enough to buy their material. If I were to caricature the typical magazine freelancer, I'd show him standing in the editor's doorway, crushing his cap between his hands while he stares at the floor and scuffs a toe into the carpet. I think many editors have the same mental image, and take advantage of this lack of self-assertiveness.

The answer is to be both professional and businesslike in your dealings with editors. If you think you deserve a raise, ask for it. Such a simple request shouldn't anger an editor, and if you've acted professionally with her in the past she's probably been expecting it. It's only good business to be paid adequately for your time and effort, just as it's good business for the publisher to get by as cheaply as possible. If the editor wants to keep using your work and you want more money, she'll usually accommodate you.

It's always possible, though, the publisher keeps such a tight hand on the pursestrings that the editor honestly can't offer more. If this is the case, the editor will tell you she's at the end of her budget. The choice of quitting or continuing to write for that publication is then up to you. These are career decisions every freelancer faces from time to time. If you're going to be a successful writer, you have to make up your mind to keep moving ahead. Allow yourself to stagnate in a low-paying market, and you'll never make enough money freelancing to turn to it on a full-time basis.

I'll never forget the first time I built up the courage to even hint that I'd like better pay. I'd been selling to this editor for two years, and in that time he'd bought maybe a dozen articles. When, in the course of a telephone conversation about a new assignment, I suggested that it might be nice to have some kind of raise, he said, "Let me see what I can do." He called back the next day, and my new rate per word amounted to a 60-percent increase over the old one!

After that experience, I soon made it a point to ask my editors to review my pay schedules on an annual basis. I did my best to make my plea in the form of a simple request, not a demand. I kept things on a businesslike level with an approach like, "It's been a year now since we last discussed money—any chance of increasing my rates for the coming year?" Nearly every business in the modern world gives annual increases to its employees, if only enough to help keep pace with the rising cost of living. The editor himself, along with all the members of his staff, is certainly expecting a somewhat fatter paycheck during the next twelve months. In point of fact you may not get your requested raise, but you're surely not going to offend anyone by asking. If an editor pleads poverty and says he simply can't grant a higher rate schedule just then, you can bet I'll remind him again in another ten or twelve months. If the answer is still no, I start thinking seriously of looking for a new editor to write for. In these days of double-digit inflation, you simply can't afford to have your purchasing power cut by 20 percent or more over a two-year time span. If an editor won't or can't give you a raise periodically, he's actually asking you to work for *less* pay every year. A working professional won't accept this kind of demotion. To do so is economic suicide.

By asking for regular increases on a more-or-less annual basis, you're putting your editors on notice that you expect to be treated as a professional. If they're professionals themselves, they'll respect you for it. What's more, by making your request an annual event you'll soon condition those editors to expect it. This makes it less of a shock to everyone concerned. I try to keep my approach light in spirit: "Well, it's time once again for my annual nagging." I try not to come across as too demanding, since a harsh confrontation is almost guaranteed to do more harm than good. At the same time, my editors know that I'm serious about the request, and that I honestly expect some kind of an adjustment—upward—in rates.

However, I don't try this tactic on editors I'm not selling to regularly. Most magazines have a basic rate they pay writers initially, and you can learn this rate by either checking *Writer's Market* or simply asking the editor. Many publications have a writer's style sheet or guide available to freelancers, and editorial rates are usually included in the information. If you submit a manuscript to a market you've never contributed to before, it's generally understood that you're willing to accept standard rate—at least initially. However, if your byline has appeared in similar publications and is familiar to your new editor, you may be able to start at substantially higher pay. If this is a possibility, you'd be wise to ask for a clarification of the magazine's payment policies when querying for the assignment. If your name is sufficiently well known. you can often start at or near the publication's top rate.

You can't allow yourself to be too pushy when querying a new editor, as you don't really have much negotiating power until he has indicated a desire to buy. If you place more emphasis on the payment expected than on selling your article idea, you'll make a poor first impression that can close doors permanently. Once he's bought a couple of your pieces, you can let him know that you consider his rates marginal and ask for a revision. But remember, you first have to prove your worth to him.

On the other hand, if a new editor calls you to offer an assignment, it's perfectly acceptable to get right down to money matters. In fact, this is an item of business that should be disposed of early in the proceedings. Once the editor has outlined the assignment and given you such details as desired length, photo support expected, and deadlines, you should start talking finances. Ask him point-blank what rates he's willing to pay. If the offer is too low, tell him exactly how much you require to do the assignment. He's coming to you, so you know in advance that he likes your work and wants to publish it in his own magazine. He also probably has a fair idea of the rates you've been working for, and he wouldn't be calling if he didn't expect to match them. So be realistic when you quote him a rate—but at the same time don't let yourself be talked down to a level you won't be satisfied with later, when you're completing the assignment. Be fair—but be firm. It's much better business to politely decline an offered assignment than to accept it grudgingly and do less than your best work in retaliation. Even if you do an outstanding job and turn in a first-class manuscript (the goal a professional writer should always strive for), you'll have weakened your bargaining position by accepting substandard pay for your work. And don't be lured by promises of better recompense "next time." If an editor can't afford your services, it's better if you both discover this as early as possible. Otherwise you're both wasting valuable time.

Another point to get straight when a new editor calls with an offer is that you consider his offer a firm, guaranteed-to-buy assignment. If there's any question about this, insist on a kill fee in the event the editor later changes his mind or simply doesn't like what you've done. This kill fee should be anywhere from one-third to one-half the agreed-upon acceptance price—and you should ask for a written agreement or contract to that effect. Regardless of the conditions agreed upon when you accept the assignment, you should ask for a written acknowledgment—and make sure you have this in hand before you begin work on the project. Editors like to make such assignments by telephone, so request written confirmation if you decide to accept. This is merely sound business practice and shouldn't offend the editor. If he *does* take offense, his motives are probably suspect. There's only one kind of businessperson who objects to putting his agreements on paper, as many writers have learned to their sorrow.

Once you have an established working relationship with an editor, such written contracts may no longer be necessary. Most freelancers eventually develop editorial contacts they regard as completely reliable, and a telephoned go-ahead is all the contract they need. Fortunately, there are still editors in the business whose word is their bond, and it's a pleasure to work with such people. It's easy to get burnt with verbal agreements, however, so unless you've developed a relationship of mutual trust with an editor, be sure you ask for confirmation of the assignment in writing. An alternative would be for you to immediately write a letter to that editor spelling out the terms of the assignment as you understand them, and asking for acknowledgment.

In addition to giving the writer legal protection, a written agreement can help prevent misunderstandings that can result from poor communication or a forgetful memory. I know I've had a few such honest misunderstandings that were resolved only when I dug my correspondence on the matter out of my files and mailed a photocopy to the editor. It's simply good insurance.

Speaking of written agreements, earlier in this chapter I mentioned the contracts many publications now demand that writers sign. These contracts spell out the publication rights the freelancer is selling, ranging from "First North American Rights Only" to "All Rights." Some contracts even refer to the assignment as a "work made for hire." If you sell all rights or sign a work-made-for-hire agreement, you lose all subsequent publication rights to the material in question. That means the magazine can turn around and resell those rights elsewhere, or republish your piece or portions of it *ad infini-*

tum without asking your permission or paying you another penny. The possibility of your article being resurrected in print may seem pretty unlikely when you sign that agreement, but it happens. I've had one of my articles republished five different times now by an editor who will best go unnamed. In this case, I sold first rights only and should have been protected from this kind of treatment. However, this happened before the 1978 revision of the copyright law, which makes my case weaker than it would be if the events were repeated today. In this particular instance, it's not worth the time and money involved to travel to New York and press suit (which is something the publisher is undoubtedly counting on). This particular company now buys all rights only, and can thus exploit writers with impunity.

Most publishers are much more honest and aren't likely to reprint an already-published article except under special circumstances. If you sell first rights only, your permission will be asked and a reprinting fee offered before the material is reused.

A more common practice is the reuse of photographs purchased with an article. If you send twenty or thirty illustrations and four or five are printed with your piece, a number of unused photos are left in the editor's file. Since most magazines purchase photos and manuscript as a single package, those extra pictures now belong to the publisher if an "all rights" agreement was signed. Magazines typically pay anywhere from $25 to $250 (or more) for one-time use of photos, and selling publication rights to photographs alone earns some freelancers a nice side income. That's another disadvantage of agreeing to an "all rights" sale.

The publishing rights offered to a magazine are usually negotiable, but some publications are becoming more insistent on purchasing all rights as a condition of the sale. If this proves to be the case, you have a decision to make: Either capitulate and sign away all rights to your work, or ask for your article back. It's up to you to decide whether the fee offered is large enough to justify relinquishing republication rights. You have to weigh the article's potential for reuse against what the magazine is willing to pay for it. Some writers refuse to sign "all rights" sales agreements as a point of principle, but as a matter of practicality you may sometimes have to give in just to make the sale. If the editor refuses to back down from a stated "all rights" policy, you may want to up the ante. If he wants your work badly enough, a compromise can usually be reached.

Just as pay rates are generally negotiable, you can often talk editors of "pay on publication" magazines into a more acceptable arrangement. Again, this is something you should consider only if you're selling to the magazine regularly, or if the editor is approaching you with an assignment. Editors are fully aware of the injustice of POP policies, and if you lobby for a change you should have a sympathetic ear. Such changes may not come about overnight, but if you persist it's possible to wear the editor down. It took me six months to nag one POP publication I used to write for into paying me on acceptance, but the editor finally tired of listening to the same argument every time we discussed an assignment over the phone. The concession was granted—along with a raise—only on the condition that I keep it strictly to myself. The publishers didn't want word to get out to other freelancers that their "inflexible" policy could actually be bent if a writer they valued was insistent enough.

If an editor firmly resists paying promptly on acceptance, he can almost always be talked into some compromise. One such arrangement I once settled for was the editor's agreement to pay within sixty days of acceptance. That particular magazine often had the piece in print within that time, and when that happened payment was actually made on publication, which allowed the editor to feel he hadn't violated his publisher's policies. What the agreement did for me was to eliminate the built-in insecurities of the standard POP contract. I knew exactly when the check would arrive, and if the editor decided to reschedule the piece for a later publishing date I didn't have to juggle my budget to accommodate his whims. Since some "pay on acceptance" markets take sixty days to get around to issuing a check, I found this two-month delay perfectly agreeable.

While a professional freelancer should continually work

with her editors to insure fair treatment—and this includes doing everything you can to treat *them* fairly in return— there's another important area of business finance no writer can long overlook. Earning top dollar for your freelancing efforts is one way to stay solvent; another is to see that you get to keep as much of that money as possible. And that brings us to the friendly folks at the Internal Revenue Service.

Income taxes will inevitably whittle away a good portion of your writing income, but freelancers enjoy certain tax benefits—or write-offs—the average nine-to-five corporate employee can't take advantage of. For instance, assignment-related travel expenses are legitimate deductions—these include mileage and/or car expenses, hotel bills, meals, tips, and other services needed while you're away from home. If you travel by bus or plane, save your ticket stubs—and remember to add in taxi fares when you arrive at your destination.

Outdoor writers can deduct hunting and fishing license fees, as well as the cost of sporting goods. Cookbook authors can write off kitchen gear and contributors to "do-it-yourself" periodicals may be able to deduct a wide assortment of tools and materials. The possibilities are endless. If you have a writing specialty that demands the use of certain equipment, you can probably deduct its full price from your tax return. The IRS uses guides and standards in determining allowable write-offs, and these are changed periodically, so it's a good idea to hire an accountant familiar with small-business taxes. Be aware that a surprising number of deductions are available to a practicing professional writer.

At one time, part-time freelancers could deduct the cost of an office at home. This deduction has been greatly restricted in recent years, and if you also work in an office away from home you may have considerable difficulty getting your basement den allowed as a write-off. Full-time freelancers can take this deduction with impunity unless they also maintain a second office elsewhere.

If you do write from home and have no other job or place of business, you can figure your deductions by comparing the floor space your office takes up with the area of the entire home, and getting a percentage. Using this figure, you can deduct that share of the monthly utility expenses, insurance, and depreciation of the home itself. (Even though every home in America is actually appreciating rapidly, the IRS allows you to depreciate the original purchase price over several years.) If, like some writers, you have a photo darkroom, this can be added to the deduction. Record- or equipment-storage areas can likewise be added to the floor-space figure, and the total annual savings can be considerable. Again, you may be wise to consult a competent accountant or tax specialist to help you determine what may or may not constitute a legal deduction.

Successful full-time writers may be able to write off the full purchase price of a car, as well as all operating expenses— gas, oil, repairs, tires, and insurance—if its operation meets certain criteria. If that car is the only vehicle the freelancer or her family owns, she may be on shaky ground trying to declare it as a business expense. But if it's not the family's sole source of transportation and the writer can show it was purchased for business use, there's an excellent chance of using it as a 100-percent write-off. There's even an investment tax credit available in the year it was purchased.

Of course, there are other day-to-day business expenses that are legal grist for the taxpayer's mill. For the freelancer, this includes typewriters, file cabinets, paper, pencils, mailing expenses—the full run of office supplies. Long-distance telephone calls, too, should be kept track of and deducted (but not if you've called Aunt Millicent in Omaha). Photography equipment—including camera, film, and processing costs—are good for yet another deduction, and some books and magazines can also come off the tax bite. The list of allowable deductions is too long to detail here, but every writer should be aware that such write-offs exist.

Even beginning writers can take full advantage of business deductions. As a matter of fact, your allowable expenses may actually exceed your writing income when you're just getting started, and this means you can declare a net business *loss*. If you do this, however, you'd better have documentation to support your claim of trying to earn part of your living as a freelancer. This can be rejection slips, assignment go-ahead letters, and other correspondence. If you've earned some actual magazine income that year, so much the better.

Because freelance writers are able to take advantage of so many tax write-offs, their returns are often subject to careful scrutiny when they're processed by the IRS. This means every writer should keep detailed records, including sales receipts, mileage tallies, and a day-to-day diary of both income earned and expenses paid. Don't be tempted to fudge a bit by failing to report some of those magazine checks, either. Publishers are required to file an earnings report with the IRS any time they pay a writer more than $600 in a single calendar year, and some magazines report any and all such income without regard to this minimum figure.

Between 10 and 15 percent of your yearly writing income can be invested in a KEOGH or IRA plan for your retirement. Taxes are deferred on income thus invested, but you usually can't touch those funds again until you reach retirement age. Your banker or financial adviser will be able to tell you about these plans.

If you intend to become a successful freelancer, you'll have to take a businesslike approach to the profession. As in every business, there are risks involved—the majority of publishers and editors are honest, but there are indeed those who operate in an unethical manner. When you have a bad experience with a publication, telephone the editor and talk things over. If you can't resolve the problem, have no further dealings with those people. You can expect to get burned every now and then; some magazines cease publication without warning and retire from the scene with wastebaskets full of unpaid bills—including fees owed to freelancers. When a publisher declares bankruptcy, all you can do is try to get in-house manuscripts returned. And if the staff has disappeared, you can't even count on this. While it's difficult for a freelancer living hundreds—even thousands—of miles away to predict a magazine's demise, there are warning signs. If a once-prompt publisher begins to fall behind in paying you, he could be experiencing cash-flow problems. If such problems pyramid, bankruptcy is likely to follow. Similarly, if several of your manuscripts pile up unpaid at some POP publisher, it may be time to call a halt until at least part of your money is forthcoming. Elusive editors who fail to answer query letters or return phone calls are sometimes another sign of impending trouble.

While bankruptcies can hurt you if a magazine goes under owing you money, they're a fact of business life and constitute a risk you must accept. A dishonest publisher who simply refuses to honor his debts is another matter entirely. Unless you live in or near the city where the publisher's offices are and can take your case to small-claims court, it may not be worth your while to press legal suit. In this case, chalk it up to experience and try to be more careful next time around.

This is where membership in a professional writers' organization can be helpful. There are a number of such groups in existence, and most circulate some kind of monthly newsletter. If a writer has difficulties with a particular publisher, she can warn other members by notifying the organization and requesting the notice be posted in the newsletter. By keeping close tabs on this early-warning system, you can avoid similar trouble by bypassing the publications listed. For a list of these organizations and their addresses, consult *Writer's Market*. These run the gamut from broad-based organizations like the Author's Guild and the National Writer's Club to such specialized groups as the Outdoor Writers' Association of America, Inc., and the Society of American Travel Writers. Membership provides association with other freelance writers and can be an important source of contacts.

If you regard writing as a simple hobby and money isn't important, you can ignore this chapter entirely. But if your motivation for writing stems even partially from need or the desire to earn a respectable income, you'd better be prepared to take a serious, businesslike approach to marketing your work. Freelancers may operate in a buyer's market, but those who are successful quickly learn to insist on fair treatment. Unless you're a good writer and businessman both, you'll never realize your full freelance earning potential. A freelance writing career can be both lucrative and satisfying, but

you must realize that it is a business and follow businesslike
guidelines to make sure your efforts reap an adequate return.
This means you must take the initiative and not rely on the
good grace of editors to determine your publishing worth.

7

Does the Boss Know You're a Writer?

Part-time freelancing is a great way to make extra money, but it *can* cause you problems with your regular job. While most employers won't object to someone on the payroll "doing a little writing" in his or her spare time, their attitude may alter dramatically when you start publishing regularly.

In the first place, some companies have definite rules regarding moonlighting, and anything you do to turn extra bucks may be flatly forbidden. If you're working for a large, impersonal corporation with inflexible rules, you may be forced to choose between freelancing and the job itself—or not being entirely honest about your after-hours activities. Since writers must eat and make mortgage payments like everyone else—and since few beginning freelancers can support themselves through manuscript sales alone—most part-time freelancers faced with this either-or condition simply omit mentioning their journalistic success at the office.

This can be difficult to do, particularly when you finally break into an important market. That first sale to a national magazine is something you'll be bursting to brag about, but if word gets around the office you may be getting a call from the personnel director. A one-time publishing effort may be ig-nored, but when your byline starts appearing with any regu-larity you can just about count on getting that call.

Whether the call brings good news or bad depends partly on the company you work for, and partly on your own em-ployment goals. If you're working in advertising, public rela-tions, or some other job where writing skills are valued, minor publishing successes may bring a pat on the back from your employer. It could even bring advancement to a more responsible position at better pay. Please note I said "minor" successes. If you're already a working journalist, advertising person, or PR hack, too much literary fame can make your immediate boss jealous or fearful. He's probably a writer, too, and if he thinks your freelance accomplishments are a threat, you've got trouble on your hands.

If you're not working at a writing or communications job, but the company that employs you has an advertising or public relations department, the call from personnel may bring an offer to move into that department. However, if you have designs on a writing position somewhere within the company, you have a much better chance of being transferred there if you initiate such a request yourself. By all means mention that you're already a selling writer when you suggest such a change. Being a published freelancer has helped some corporation employees sidestep the usual college-degree re-quirements PR and advertising jobs typically have. The abil-ity to write, and write well, is considered rare in most cor-porate circles, and if your company's personnel people are on the ball they'll take advantage of your proven copywriting skills. This won't always happen, but it's a possibility worth considering.

If you're a factory or construction worker, you may have little opportunity to capitalize on your writing skills and im-prove your employment outlook. However, a blue-collar boss is more likely to look upon your writing as mere dilettantism, and therefore express no objection.

If your boss learns you're a publishing writer and realizes it's not affecting your work at the office, he may simply con-gratulate you and let it go at that. However, any money-making activity engaged in at home is automatically suspect by most employers. Obviously, you're spending time at the endeavor—and most companies feel they have a vested interest in how you use your spare time. If may not seem fair, but that's often the case. They reason that since you need to spend a certain amount of time with your family each day in addition to eating and sleeping, you may be robbing yourself of needed rest in order to freelance. If you have time left over from the above activities, you're supposed to jog, play tennis, or participate in other healthful recreation to keep physically fit.

This is why many companies have firm rules against moonlighting of any kind. And as I've pointed out, an employer may overlook unsuccessful freelancing efforts as a hobby, but take a very different attitude when your byline appears regularly on the magazine stands.

Another problem you'll eventually face as editors begin using more of your material is that they'll one day start calling you with assignments, or to discuss a problem with your latest manuscript. While it can be flattering to have an editor telephone, it can quickly create difficulties if he calls you at work. But how else can he contact you during business hours?

If you have a desk job and your own telephone extension, you can hide a few such calls from your boss's scrutiny. But as you come closer to being a steadily publishing writer, this will become more and more difficult. The day will come when your boss confronts you with all the time you're spending on the telephone. Of course, your problem is even more serious if you have to be paged to answer the phone.

It can be embarrassing to ask an editor to stop calling you at work, but this may prove necessary to save your job. Most editors are understanding about this, as the majority of freelancers hold some other job and write in their spare time. You might consider an arrangement that once worked for me while I was employed by a company unsympathetic to my literary yearnings. I asked my wife not to relay my office phone number to editors unless it was absolutely necessary for them to reach me immediately. Instead, she would take any message the caller cared to leave, and assure him I would call back later the same day. I made it a habit to call home during the lunch hour to collect such messages, and then used my telephone credit card to return the calls before it was time to go back to work.

You can also use time-zone differences to your advantage. I live in the Mountain zone, and before I turned to freelancing full-time I tried to do most of my telephoning to New York City publishing houses in the morning before I left for work. By placing my calls before 8:00 a.m., I didn't intrude on my employer's time, and also got the benefit of much cheaper rates. By the same token, calls to West Coast editors could often be deferred until after work—and again, the rates are lower after 5:00 p.m.

It goes without saying that you should never steal company time to write freelance copy. In addition to being dishonest, participation in this kind of illicit activity is practically begging for the chance to collect unemployment. It's bad enough that your boss—or even *his* boss—suspects freelancing is affecting your work. Give them concrete evidence, and your goose is ready for the carving knife. I've known a few advertising copywriters who succumbed to the temptation to dash out "just a few lines" while on the job, and in most cases the practice eventually caught up with them. Don't do it! If it's a slow day at the office and you have nothing to do, it's safer to goof off than work on a magazine assignment. Employers expect you to waste a bit of time now and then, but they *don't* expect to catch you with outside work in your typewriter.

If you're fortunate enough to work for a boss who appreciates proven writing talent, you'll want to bend over backward to make sure he knows he's getting his money's worth keeping you on the payroll. At the same time, it can be hazardous to show copies of your latest articles around the office, or even mention them to your supervisor. This form of bragging is seldom appreciated. What's more, it can disrupt a busy office schedule, and if the boss once too often catches his secretary reading your deathless prose instead of typing letters, he may begin questioning your worth to the organization.

Advertising your freelancing success can create jealousies

that may haunt you later on. Not everyone in the office will be tickled by your good fortune, and if your supervisor happens to be a writer, too, you can have problems. When I first began selling to magazines, I made the mistake of bringing the first several published articles to the office to impress the boss. He was a writer himself, and in fact held a Pulitzer Prize for journalism won in his younger days as a newspaper reporter. The thought of making him jealous never entered my mind. I may not actually have had that effect on him, but I do know our relationship changed for the worse after I started showing him magazines with my byline in them. I later learned he had recently accumulated a few rejection slips for freelancing efforts of his own, and the turndowns didn't sit well. Since he was moonlighting, too, he didn't say much about my after-hours activities—but I had certainly picked a poor time to point out my literary achievements. Writers can be a pretty temperamental lot, and the smart freelancer surrounded by similarly talented types at work will do her best to avoid ruffling feathers in the office. Keeping a low profile can be prudent practice.

If you earn the bulk of your living as an advertising copywriter, writing teacher, editor, or PR person, a list of published credits makes a great addition to your résumé when you're changing jobs. Such a list proves your professional competence, particularly if the names of some readily recognizable national magazines appear on it. A successful freelancing effort can be a big help to the writer on the move, and a handful of tear sheets can give you a snug lead over other writers you may be competing with.

Paradoxically, the company that hires you *because* of past publishing achievement may make a 180-degree change in attitude about your freelancing once you're hired. This happened to me when I signed on as the advertising and public relations manager of an international manufacturing concern. When I applied for the job, they couldn't have been more pleased about the number of times my byline had appeared in national publications. I was just what they were looking for, they said. They wanted someone with proven initiative, and a self-starter who could put words in print in a professional, readable manner was exactly the right man for the company.

The problem arose when I continued to freelance after signing on. Before accepting the job, I had informed both the personnel manager and the vice-president of my intention to do just that, but it wasn't too many months later that the VP called me into his office for a heart-to-heart chat. The thrust of the conversation was that while the company didn't *really* object to my writing a freelance magazine piece every six months or so, I probably wasn't going to have enough spare time to remain a regular contributor to any magazine. Too, the company was concerned that I might eventually decide to become a full-time freelancer (shrewd fellows!). They didn't want to invest four or five years in "training" me for my job, only to have me assert my independence one day.

Essentially, what they wanted was for me to quit my freelancing, and at the same time assure the company of my undying loyalty and fidelity until the day I was handed a gold watch and my retirement papers. Such a request was ridiculous on the face of it, particularly since people in advertising seldom stay on the same job or with the same employer many years at a time. It's a particularly mobile profession, to use a popular euphemism for job hopping, and few people in it are willing to spend an entire career at the same desk.

However, the fact that my byline appeared in magazines with some frequency worried them. Independence was something that could be carried too far; it runs against the corporate grain.

While I assured my boss that I had no intention of jumping ship in the foreseeable future, I also informed him I just couldn't afford to stop freelancing unless the company wanted to increase my salary 50 percent. By that time, the extra income had become an economic necessity. We had several such talks in later months, and eventually the corporation and I parted company.

I don't mean to imply that freelancing will necessarily cause you problems with your job anywhere you may be employed. I worked in the public relations department of a large utility for more than seven years, and my freelancing bothered no one. I was even given leaves of absence to cover travel assignments, and the company president subscribed to one magazine I was a monthly contributor to. It just happened that my superiors there displayed tolerant understanding of my after-hours activities, and as long as nothing interfered with my work at the office no objections were raised. If anything, my publishing success added to my employment stature.

Although writing feature articles for magazines requires a different technique than that used to create advertising copy or crank out press releases, many companies see a real benefit in having a magazine writer handy. I've helped polish an engineer's jargon-ridden prose for publication in a trade journal, ghosted articles for company executives, and written more than a few speeches. I've even edited a couple of company publications—and this usually means doing all the writing, photo-taking, editing, and layout work yourself. If a company has any of these chores on tap, they'll be ecstatic about your magazine background.

Annual reports require the same storytelling skills you develop whenever you write for publication; if you can make one of these deadly tomes more readable you can earn substantial praise. Executive bulletins may also profit by your expertise, and dividend enclosures or other shareholder communications often require a more sophisticated touch than the executive in charge can give them. In addition, the personnel department can sometimes use help in writing employee-benefit booklets and other informational handouts. Even if your company lacks an advertising or public relations department, there are many areas in which you can apply your writing skills.

The point is, your employer can usually turn your freelancing abilities to her own advantage, if she'll just stop to think about it. The fact that you moonlight may suddenly become less objectionable if your boss sees that the company can gain from it. If she disapproves of your after-hours publishing pursuits, point out how your writing capability can be turned to your employer's advantage.

If you have a job you don't want to give up, and your

employer not only learns that you're freelancing but stren-
uously objects, there's another option you might consider. If
that part-time magazine income isn't substantial enough to
risk losing your job over, you can always go into semiretire-
ment as far as periodicals are concerned—and try writing a
book. I'll discuss book authorship further in chapter 9, but let
me point out a few advantages of turning to a book-length
project when in the above predicament.

In the first place, you can truthfully tell your boss you've
given up (at least temporarily) your freelance magazine writing pursuits. By thus giving in, you can mollify your employer
and keep that steady salary flowing. Until your freelancing
becomes lucrative enough to sustain you in your accustomed
style, a regular paycheck is nothing to walk away from ca-
sually. You may *never* want to abandon this kind of security,
in fact, so keep your options open.

It may take several months to land a nonfiction book contract, and if you're working on a first novel you may have to
write the entire thing on speculation before seeing any spend-
able cash. In some ways, a first book is like that first magazine article you sold. You have to prove yourself at least
once—but after that, subsequent assignments become easier
to get.

Regardless of whether you elect to write book-length nonfiction or a novel, this is the kind of project you can easily
hide from the boss. Your name won't be appearing on the
newsstands each month, and coworkers can't embarrass you
by waving your latest published piece around the office.
Furthermore, the loss of your moonlighting income may leave
you looking hungrier and shabbier, and you may be able to
promote yourself a small raise in consideration of your sacri-
fice.

Just keep your mouth shut about that book you're working
on. Don't air the plot to coworkers, or even mention your
project to those who might spread the word. Even if your boss
should learn of your new after-hours endeavor, few people
take would-be book authors seriously. Call it a hobby that
gives you something to do with your time.

If and when your book finally sees print, you may be in a

better position to evaluate alternatives if publication once again angers your boss. You've kept your promise to swear off magazines, so there should be no real ground for complaint—and nine times out of ten there won't be any outraged objections raised. Somehow, writing a book seems less of a legitimate part-time job, and most employers won't feel threatened by this kind of undertaking. But if your book *does* cause trouble at work, you may have the last laugh. A first book-writing effort may net you only $3,000 or $4,000 in advances, possibly even less. But lightning does sometimes strike. A friend of mine started writing her very first novel a couple of years ago, and when it finally sold the advance check totaled $40,000! If you're earning $15,000 or $20,000 at your regular job, the prospect of losing it would certainly be less threatening with this kind of assurance in your pocket.

You can't count on that kind of fortune. But even without a huge first advance, writing books may ultimately prove more profitable than competing in the magazine market. If a book is successful enough to support several printings, royalties can amount to several thousand dollars during the lifetime of the book. As long as it remains in print, royalties should continue to trickle in—and this is money you don't have to do anything more to earn. All you have to do is cash the checks as they arrive.

If you manage to get several different books into print, and royalties accrue from all of them, that income can start adding up. There are other possibilities, too, for additional income from those one-time efforts—paperback rights, book club selections, and even foreign sales. If you've written a novel that catches the right eye, there may even be motion-picture rights to negotiate.

So even if your boss demands you give up freelancing as a condition of employment, you can honor your commitment without giving up writing entirely. Few would equate regular freelancing with part-time book authorship, although the latter may earn more money in the long run.

Does your boss know you're a writer? And if he does, will it make any difference to him or the job? Unless you're sure of the answer, it may be best to do your freelancing quietly without drawing attention to it at the office. You'll have to be the judge of whether freelancing will help or hinder your regular nine-to-five career if the secret leaks out.

Expand
Your
Writing
Income

Writing magazine articles and authoring books aren't the only ways a freelancer can earn money. There are numerous writing assignments up for grabs in every moderate-sized city, and some of these pay very well.

There are brochures to be written, advertisements to be created, and news releases to type and distribute. Business executives need speeches written for them, or professional help with sales letters and other literature.

Advertising, promotion, public relations, and speechwriting are only a few areas in which businesses need skilled writing help. Many manufacturers pack instructional booklets along with their products, while others require support material for their salespeople. Annual reports must be published each year, and employee newspapers or company magazines are commonplace in the corporate world.

Sales films must be written before they're produced, and there are company histories, dividend enclosures, and catalogs that need the attention of professional writers. The list is endless, presenting the freelancer with diverse (and sometimes highly profitable) possibilities.

Business corporations aren't the only places a writer can

peddle his skills. Sometimes private individuals are willing to pay professionals to ghost articles or books. Many family-run organizations want their histories chronicled in print; some will pay for genealogical research and reporting.

Politicians need vote-luring speeches written, and during a hot campaign may hire numerous writers and publicity people. Local government organizations often employ public relations people on a part-time basis, and nonprofit organizations and foundations are always seeking effective grant writers.

Check out local colleges and universities. These institutions have the same writing and public relations requirements businesses have, along with other possibilities. You may find yourself teaching an adult education course in writing, or even winning a place on the regular faculty.

These are but a few of the money-making options open to professional writers. I should point out, though, that these don't strictly fit the popular image of a freelancer. Writing news releases and advertising copy is pretty mundane stuff to someone hungering to see his byline in *The New Yorker* or *Playboy*. Furthermore, you'll never get rich doing these jobs on a part-time—or even full-time—basis. You can earn enough to pay the rent, and perhaps support yourself in modest style. But you can forget about best-seller royalties and motion-picture rights. You'll be selling your time by the hour or week. If you're freelancing full-time and have no other means of support, this money can be most welcome—particularly when you're first starting out and haven't yet managed to stabilize your magazine- or book-writing income. It's possible to charge a respectable hourly rate or work on a piecemeal basis and generate enough cash flow to keep your creditors happy and food on the table.

One common error made by many new writers is the failure to charge *enough* for a writing project. If you're working for a flat hourly rate, don't be afraid to include time spent meeting with the client, researching, and rewriting to the client's specifications after the original work is completed. I hesitate to suggest an hourly rate because some writers are faster and more proficient than others, and the cost of writ-

ing, like the cost of living, varies dramatically with geo-
graphic locale. However, twenty dollars an hour certainly
isn't out of line, and some freelancers charge more than twice
that with impunity.

If you're charging a flat fee for the job, be sure to set the
price high enough to cover *all* the time you'll be spending on
the project. Remember, too, that a fast writer who does consistently good work is justified in charging a higher hourly
rate than a slower wordsmith.

If you already have a steady nine-to-five job and are freelancing part-time, stop and think twice before spending time
drumming up advertising or PR business. If you find you
enjoy this work, well and good. But if that's the case, you
should strive for a full-time publicity job with some company
and use your spare time for freelance magazine- and book-
writing efforts. If you already have such a job, moonlighting
in the same field—particularly if you work for people in competition with your regular employer—could cause serious re-
percussions.

In other words, it's possible to earn a good hourly wage as a
freelance advertising writer or public relations person, but
it's easy to let this activity fill all your spare time. Not that
there's anything wrong with that, but it won't get magazine
articles or book-length manuscripts written and sold. Such
"writer for hire" tactics are often necessary for the full-time
freelancer, and it's a darned good thing these jobs are available. But I think it's a mistake for the budding freelancer already holding a legitimate job to pursue such assignments—at
least if he's serious about becoming a successful magazine
contributor or book author. Pandering to someone's corporate image can be tempting if the pay is right, but it doesn't
take you far toward professional authorship. You should decide early what your goals are, and act accordingly.

Now that I've unburdened myself of that advice, let's see
how you can land some of these less glamorous writing assignments. The first thing you must realize is that most large
companies—and many smaller ones—already have full-time
advertising and public relations staffs. Or they may simply
have an executive in charge of those functions who hires an

outside agency to do the actual work. This is the normal arrangement; it can constitute a sizable stumbling block to your plans.

One way to skirt the problem is to find out which advertising or public relations agency the company employs, and then approach the agency itself for part-time copywriting work. Most advertising organizations are chronically short of creative people, and there's often work the account executive would gladly farm out. Take samples of your published writing and anything else you can lay your hands on to impress him with your professionalism. Make it clear that you're looking for *part-time* work, and that you can be depended upon to meet tight deadlines if need be. The advertising game is an up-and-down proposition, and the agency is usually either overstaffed or understaffed at any given time. Having a skilled part-time writer on tap can be highly helpful, particularly to a relatively small agency. Because you're not a regular staff member, you draw no weekly salary and require no expensive health insurance, vacation, and retirement benefits—in short, you're not part of the regular overhead. Unlike the agency's other employees, the only time you run up any payroll expense is when you're actually working on a project—and since your fee is automatically passed along to the client, you don't really cost the agency anything at all.

If you can produce copy that keeps the client happy, the agency will be ecstatic. If this happens, you can look for an increasing number of assignments. Add the published clippings to your portfolio, and you can peddle your talent to other agencies as well.

Let's take a second to touch on that portfolio. In essence, your collection of published ads, magazine articles, and other work serves as your professional introduction. It's your sole proof that you know what you're doing when you sit behind a typewriter, and without it you have only a marginal chance of landing a business-writing assignment. So make your portfolio as professional-looking as possible. Tear sheets shouldn't really be torn from magazines, but carefully cut and preserved between plastic covers. Ad layouts should be mounted on cardboard, under plastic. Radio or television commercial scripts should be neatly typed on the appropriate forms. If you've published full-length features in well-known periodicals, leave the magazines intact rather than excising your articles for individual presentation. This gives your work added impact, particularly if it appeared in recent issues and warranted multi-page treatment. However, don't overdo by toting a suitcase full of back issues to an interview. Select your best work if you have a big batch to choose from, and present it in a single attractive package. A loose-leaf folder is one possibility, or it may be handier to use a large artist's envelope to keep your work together. The latter is particularly useful if the materials you have are on different-sized sheets.

A simple business card with your name, address, and telephone number is an excellent investment when you're looking for freelance copywriting work. If you've spent a few extra dollars to have a professional-looking logo added to the card, better yet. First impressions count heavily, and if you can't sell yourself with a little snazzy packaging, the agency won't think much of your creative ability. Incidentally, don't stop with the card. Once the artwork is done, you may as well go ahead and have stationery printed, too. This can be used for billing the agency as each assignment is completed (don't overlook this final step, or you may be a while collecting your money), as well as for other business correspondence. I've already noted in chapter 3 that a professional-looking letterhead can help sell article queries; the same holds true for advertising and PR writing assignments. If the letterhead identifies you as simply a "writer," you can use the same stationery for both kinds of freelancing.

While most medium- to large-sized businesses have their own advertising and PR departments or hire outside agencies to do this work, many smaller firms have no permanent publicity arrangements. It costs money to staff even a one-person advertising office, and most independent agencies want a monthly guarantee or retainer from their clients. Therefore, smaller businesses are often receptive to freelance proposals. You can offer to work on a piecework basis to turn out news releases and similar communications. And don't stop when you've written the release—see that it's delivered to the business editors of all local newpapers, and radio and television stations as well if the story is sufficiently newsworthy to interest the electronic media. When the release sees print, make sure the person who hired you gets copies of the published piece. Such tactics help prove your worth, and repeat business comes from satisfied customers.

Once you have a working relationship with a company, it should be a simple matter to promote other assignments. Offer to write any advertising copy the firm might need. If the company does enough advertising, or if you develop several small ad accounts among various businesses, it might pay to have a second letterhead printed up identifying yourself as an advertising agency. (This may also require incorporation, so check your state's business laws.) That way you can place your ads under agency aegis and collect the standard 15-percent commission on space rates. When you have agency status, your client normally pays its media bills through you, and you simply deduct your commission when paying the newspaper, magazine, or broadcasting station. In effect, the media pay your fee (the 15-percent commission) and your client receives your services free. The danger here is that the media will then direct the bills to you, rather than to the company you're placing the ads for. If the company reneges, you'll be stuck for the payment.

Offer to write the company's annual report. Find out when this report is usually mailed, and get started on it several months early. Be sure to find out exactly what preparing the report will entail. If the project you're tackling is a large one that must meet Securities and Exchange Commission (SEC) requirements, you'd better quote a price high enough to net a decent profit on your time. If you've never written an annual report, study the company's reports for the past few years to see what work is involved. (A helpful reference work is David F. Hawkins's *Corporate Financial Reporting*, Irwin Publishing, 1818 Ridge Road, Homewood IL 60430.) If the project promises to be a lengthy one, you might be wise to do the work on an hourly basis rather than bid a flat fee for the job.

How much should you charge for your business-writing

work? There's really no set fee, so you must decide what your time is worth—and then balance this against the company's ability or willingness to pay. Don't undervalue the work you do. Many freelancers earn forty to fifty dollars an hour for time actually spent writing magazine manuscripts, and charge only slightly less than that for business assignments. Remember, plumbers and electricians average more than twelve dollars an hour in many areas, and your creative work should be worth more than that. If it isn't, maybe you'd better trade your typewriter for a pipe wrench.

When writing freelance advertising copy for an agency, you should probably charge somewhere in the neighborhood of fifteen to thirty-five dollars an hour, depending on the area you live in and how flush the agency's budget is. In metropolitan areas you can charge more than you could get away with in some smaller town in the Midwest. When you're selling directly to the client, you can probably boost your rates a bit, since no charges will be added by a go-between agency. As you become more experienced and find yourself in greater demand, you can adjust your fee schedule accordingly—upward, of course.

News-release writing can be charged for on the same hourly basis, or you can contract for this work piecemeal and charge a flat fee for each release as it's distributed. Newspaper advertisements—including "help wanted" ads to attract new employees—can be handled the same way. Again, the prices charged depend on what the traffic will bear, and on how little you're willing to work for. Just remember, as a freelance contractor you set the price. If you find yourself underpaid, you'll have no one else to blame.

While day-to-day news releases about company plans, promotions, and other events to be covered in local newspapers should be written for minimum rates—say fifteen or twenty dollars an hour, or a thirty-dollar flat fee—new-product releases are an entirely different thing. These are a form of advertising, and such releases will be widely distributed. It requires more skill to write an effective new-product announcement, and should be charged for accordingly. Many writers ask three hundred to five hundred dollars apiece for a one- or two-page release, including writing and distribution. Reproduction and postage costs are charged for separately.

Whenever you agree to do any industrial writing, remember to assess for the time you spend in conference and interviewing people, as well as actual writing. And if you're embarking on a lengthy project like an annual report or company history, you should ask for a reasonable retainer in advance. If you're doing the job for a flat fee, anywhere from one-third to one-half the money should be paid up front, with the remainder due on delivery of the finished piece. Be sure to get the terms of the agreement in writing, with the due date and financial arrangements clearly spelled out. This is the only businesslike way to handle major writing jobs, and your client shouldn't object to such a contract, as it protects you both.

Writing speeches for company executives should be approached in a similar manner. Speechwriting properly done is a highly refined art and should be charged for accordingly. Typical fees run from three hundred to three thousand dollars, depending on who your client is and to whom the speech will be made. The length of the speech also affects price, although most business talks take between fifteen and twenty-five minutes to deliver.

Like other writing, speechwriting is a specialty that must be learned through practice. Remember that your script will be spoken, not merely read. Words and phrases that look good in print may sound awkward and stilted during vocal delivery. The only way to see what works is to read everything you write aloud—or better yet, have someone else read the script to you while you listen. Be on the watch for words that are difficult to pronounce, or sibilants that sound like an assembly of snakes (read that last line into a microphone to see what I mean). Membership in Toastmasters or a similar public-speaking organization may also prove helpful, and is tax-deductible.

And remember, the speech shouldn't sound like it was written by you. It must bear the unmistakable stamp of your client, because most (make that *all*) executives want to take full credit for the speeches they deliver. You're actually ghosting the speech and should never advertise that you were its real author. This is another reason you should charge a reasonably high fee: it's the only recognition you'll receive from the job. How do you earmark a speech you've written to indelibly identify it with your client? One way is to listen for favored catchwords or phrases as you interview the executive. Everyone has pet words he habitually uses—and often overuses— and if you're alert these should quickly become apparent to you. Simply make sure you sprinkle a few of these tidbits around in the text, and the exec's friends and business acquaintances are sure to pick up on these subtle clues.

Another way to learn more about the client's normal style of expression is to read over some of his or her day-to-day business correspondence or memos. Most executives are forced to do a certain amount of writing each day, even if it is accomplished through dictation. Again, watch for key words and phrases that keep popping up. This exercise will also give you a general feeling for the client's vocabulary and verbal sophistication. It's easy to write a speech that's too smoothly urbane, and if it's obviously out of step with the man's or woman's normal style you'll end up making the client look ridiculous. That's hardly the way to encourage repeat business.

Speaking of ghostwriting, many high-powered executives are willing to pay handsome rates to have articles—or even books—you write published under their names. Physicians and other professionals are another market for this kind of work. These people feel that publishing will enhance their professional reputations, and even if that isn't always true, their egos may simply need feeding. To handle such assignments successfully, you'll be forced to do considerable research to write authoritatively on the subject the client selects. This may mean contacting other authorities in your client's particular area of expertise. If this proves necessary, don't let those you talk with know you're working as a ghost. Always maintain the client's confidentiality.

So how do you advertise your availability as a ghostwriter? Once you've pleased a few clients, word will get around.

Executives you've worked for will often recommend you to colleagues who need "help" with their writing. This euphemistic attitude may be maintained throughout your relationship with a client, even though it's tacitly understood by both parties that you'll be ghosting the whole project on your own. The client will probably make a few specific suggestions that you should do your best to adopt, but otherwise you're likely to be left pretty much on your own. You may also be asked to edit a manuscript the client has already written to "whip it into shape" for publication. Such projects can be touchy, particularly if extensive rewriting is required. You have to be both an editor and a diplomat as you explain the changes to be made. Many people become very proprietary about words they've written down, and their egos may not fare well under professional editing. My advice is to accept such jobs at your own risk—and be sure to make it very clear that drastic copy changes may be required if the manuscript is to have any hope of seeing print. If you think the whole idea is a lost cause and the subject matter is probably unpublishable in any form, you'll be better off turning the assignment down.

The best way to get started as a professional ghostwriter is to call on potential clients and let them know of your availability. Be sure to leave your business card at the end of the visit. Some ghosts advertise occasionally in the classified ads, but if you acquire clients in this manner make sure you get a healthy cash advance before beginning their projects. Such ads bring a lot of weirdos out of the woodwork, and you can waste a lot of valuable time sorting legitimate inquiries from those made by people who may not be playing with a full deck. To avoid getting lost in the shuffle, sort out the less serious in advance with a quick phone call. If a subsequent meeting appears in order, you should first make it clear that you work under contract with a cash advance. Promises to "pay when it's done" should be discounted from the start, and would-be authors who offer to split the proceeds resulting from their once-in-a-lifetime ideas must be given a polite but firm "no thanks."

When talking with companies about possible assignments,

be sure to inquire about the communication they maintain with their employees. Most medium-to-large businesses support an employee newsletter or some other house organ; if your client company lacks such a means of in-house communication, it may be ripe for your suggestions. Again, charge according to the size and frequency of the publication, making sure it's clearly understood that your fees are in addition to all production and distribution costs. How much should you charge? You can assess your usual hourly rate, or simply charge a flat rate for each issue. This can run from two hundred to two thousand dollars or more at a crack, depending on the work involved.

Motion-picture scriptwriting is another possibility: many companies commission promotional films. You might consider teaming up with a freelance cinematographer to offer a complete package deal. Industrial filmwriting is much less demanding than the scriptwork Hollywood requires, but if you've never attempted this kind of enterprise I'd advise checking one of the larger libraries in your area for a book on the subject. The basics are actually easy to learn, but you must think visually rather than in terms of words alone. The toughest part of the job is to plan the images that will appear in the film, and make sure they appear in a logical, smooth-flowing sequence. Don't overdo the dialogue. A mistake most beginners make is to jam the film with verbiage. Pauses in the narration are needed for relief, and you should frequently remind yourself that you're working in a visual medium. The pictures should do most of the work.

One last comment about film work: If you'll be working with a cinematographer on an all-inclusive single-bid basis, be sure to budget enough to hire an experienced film editor. You'll need a narrator, too, and his services can come surprisingly high. Don't try to skimp by hiring some relative with a super-rich voice unless he's also a professional performer. An amateur delivery is easy to spot, and can destroy the effect of the entire film. Here's a hint: Local radio announcers are often available for reasonable fees, and a good one can give your product the professional touch it so vitally needs.

Slide presentations are much less demanding than film

scripts, although the same basic principles apply. You can do your own picture editing, and you can even make substantial script changes after all the photographs have been shot. Because slide shows are much less costly than sound-on-film presentations, they are easier to sell to small businesses. Keep this in mind when making your pitch for freelance assignments.

If you have an engineering or physical science background, you should have little trouble finding freelance technical writing assignments. Such jobs typically include instructional brochures, specification sheets, and work proposals, although there are many other projects a freelancer may work on. In some large cities there are temporary-help agencies that place technical writers in short-term jobs on a fee-splitting basis. Before you sign up for such work, be sure you understand the hourly rates usually offered. By the time the agency takes its cut, you may not be willing to work for the remainder.

Once you've sold a few articles to magazines or had a book published, you may be able to find part-time work teaching an adult education or college creative writing class. Many of these courses are taught at night, and can provide small but steady side income. More importantly, they bring you in contact with a variety of people and ideas. Writing can be a lonely trade, as you spend several hours each day with only your typewriter and thesaurus for company. You can easily become isolated from the world around you, particularly when working on a book-length assignment and trying simultaneously to juggle various magazine deadlines. A couple of hours each week spent in front of a writing class can help clear away the cobwebs and keep you in touch with reality.

Another possibility lies in convincing the local newspaper that your weekly column on gardening, cooking, photography, or some other specialty would be well received by readers. But be prepared for a shock unless you're talking with the editor of a large metropolitan daily—newspaper copy rates leave much to be desired, and you'll never pay for that Porsche with column earnings unless lightning strikes and you become nationally syndicated. However, it's a few extra bucks each month, and those bylined columns can help pad your portfolio. If you write a travel column, you may find yourself being offered a surprising variety of all-expense-paid trips to exotic destinations. One of my close friends writes a weekly outdoors column for that reason alone. The pay isn't much, but the fringes can be fantastic.

The opportunities for freelance writing work right in your own community are literally endless. Everyone—businesses and governments included—needs to communicate, and a professional writer does that job better than most people can. You may need to exercise a little imagination and ingenuity to get word of your abilities around to potential employers, but it's really not all that difficult. Just conduct yourself professionally and charge rates you can live with. If you sell your services too cheaply they won't be respected. The beginner often errs by budget-pricing her work for fear of losing assignments. Don't fall into this trap. Set your rates at an intelligent level, and stick with them. Remember what a journeyman plumber charges, and don't let yourself be talked into accepting wages his apprentice would spurn. The only way to be treated as a professional in any trade is to act like one—and that means insisting on fair recompense for your labors.

Finally, don't lose sight of your long-range writing goals. There's nothing wrong with writing advertising or public relations copy to supplement your regular freelance income, but most writers gain more satisfaction from seeing their bylines in national print or on the jacket of a newly published book. The kind of full financial freedom that accompanies sought-for success in the publishing field can be a long time coming, and indeed may never become a reality. But it remains a goal worth reaching for.

Writing
Your
First
Book

Magazine articles are fun, fast, and reasonably rewarding, but sooner or later nearly every free-lancer wants to write a book. The ideal time to tackle this project is while you're still freelancing part-time—your success or failure could help you decide whether or not to become a full-time writer later on.

In chapter 12 I'll explain in detail why book authorship is vitally important to full-time professionals. For the moment, please accept this as fact: If you have serious intentions of becoming a financially successful writer, you may as well start planning that very first book. This advice holds even if you remain a part-time freelancer the rest of your life. Writing for magazines—even top-paying, prestigious publications—will never give you more than a month-to-month income. That monthly cash flow can be pretty satisfying and may even let you keep current on all your bills with a few bucks to spare. But pay from the periodicals won't make you rich, and ends the moment you quit turning out those 2,000-word manuscripts.

Writing a book may not make you rich, either, but if you go about it right—and get lucky—you can realize a heftier cash return by writing a 70,000-word book than you'd get from thirty-five separate magazine-length features. This doesn't always happen, but the possibility is there. If a book sells well it can make many thousands of dollars for its author, and the money keeps rolling in as long as the book remains in print.

In addition to collecting royalties, a book can generate extra earnings through foreign rights sales if a publisher in some other country wants it on his list. A more common occurrence is for a paperback publisher to pick up on a reasonably successful hardcover title (assuming the book was first printed as a clothbound edition). When this happens, the initial sale of paperback rights can give the writer a quick cash boost, and subsequent softcover royalties can be similarly welcome. You may be splitting some of the proceeds with the original publisher, depending on the terms of your contract, but even so the sale of other rights can provide a healthy bonanza—and without requiring any extra effort from the freelancer.

If you've written a successful novel, there's always the chance of receiving a six-figure bonus from the motion-picture people, or your book may even be adapted to television. Such occurrences form the substance of an author's fantasies, and many writers never earn a nickel beyond the publisher's initial advance. However, books have made some authors rich almost overnight. Simply having your title selected by a book club can leave you with enough ready cash to pay off the mortgage and take a whirlwind tour of Europe. Statistically speaking, first novels aren't regarded as moneymakers. It usually takes a novelist a couple of different books to hit his or her stride, so you shouldn't quit your office job on the strength of a publisher's acceptance letter, or even a contract. However, lightning does strike every once in a while—as a case in point, I know a young woman who started writing just three years ago. Her very first book—a historical romance—sold the second time out, netting a fat $40,000 advance. In addition, the publishers who purchased it have offered a multi-book contract for subsequent work, with an escalating advance scale. At this writing, my friend and her husband are touring China to obtain background material for the next novel in the series.

While such success is definitely the exception to the rule for new novelists, it *can* happen. But the possibility doesn't even *exist* until you write that first book. Magazine writers seeking real financial security are similar to those people who daydream about winning a million bucks in the Irish Sweepstakes—but never bother to buy a ticket. Books have by far the greatest potential for substantial cash return, and the freelancer who ignores this market is crippling himself financially.

Novels may represent the golden ring on the writer's carrousel, but nonfiction books can be equally rewarding. Nonfiction is often easier to write, since dialogue, characterization, and plot needn't be bothered with. What's more, you can usually sell a well-thought-out how-to or self-help book on the basis of a relatively brief proposal—which means you get a contract and cash advance *before* the book is written. This eliminates much of the risk in spending months on a book-length project. Most writers find it easier to concentrate when they know their work is presold, and having a little money up front helps you survive while the book is in progress.

Because more publishers print nonfiction than fiction these days, you have a better chance of finding a market for your first book if it's something other than a novel. Let's leave volumes of poetry out of the discussion, as their success ratio is so dismal I can't imagine any freelancer who needs money even considering such a project. I'm *not* saying your first book *shouldn't* be a novel. If writing fiction has greater appeal and is what you really want to do, so be it. You may get lucky and cash in big right from the start. But remember that the odds for your first book are better in one of the nonfiction fields.

With that in mind, let's see what you should do to get that initial book sold and under way. Obviously, the first thing you need is an idea or concept. Since ideas are a writer's stock in trade, coming up with a half-dozen or so nonfiction book possibilities shouldn't be too much of a problem if you'll only take a few days to think the matter over. Unfortunately, there are often differences between what constitutes a *good* book idea and a concept with commercial possibilities.

When searching your psyche for a nonfiction subject, you should ask yourself, "What do I know that others will be willing to pay ten to twelve dollars to learn?" If that draws a blank, ask instead, "What am I interested in, and maybe know a little about, that would greatly interest others?" You don't have to be a fount of knowledge about a subject to write authoritatively on it. If you're willing to do the necessary research, there'll be very few topics you won't be able to handle. A good friend of mine boasts that he'd even tackle a book on *Brain Surgery, Self-Taught* if the money was right and the deadline distant enough to allow him to read up on the subject.

While many full-time professionals feel much the same way, you may encounter problems if you stray too far from familiar ground. In the first place, any publisher will want to see your credentials if you propose a book that requires special expertise. This is one reason it's wise to select a subject you have at least a nodding acquaintance with. If you've published a couple of dozen articles about home gardening, you'll have an easier time convincing a publisher you can deliver a book titled *Better Beet-Growing in Your Backyard.* Having the proper writing background is particularly important when you're trying to land your first book contract. Until you've actually published a book, you represent an unknown quantity to acquisition editors. Regular sales to the magazine market aren't a guarantee that you have the skill and perseverance to successfully complete a book-length project. Successful completion implies meeting the contract deadline with a competently written, ready-for-publication manuscript. It requires a different kind of discipline to stick with a 275-page enterprise than it takes to turn out a 2,000-word feature.

With that in mind, try to think of a subject in which you can demonstrate a degree of expertise. This isn't an absolute must (there are few absolutes in publishing), but it's likely to go a long way toward interesting an editor in the project.

If you've done your homework and scanned the shelves of your local bookstore, you'll have a pretty good idea of the kind of subjects that sell: Self-help books probably lead the current list, so if you can tell people how to lose weight, make more money, be more popular, or have a better sex life, you're on the right track. One problem you may encounter with a self-help title is a lack of professional credentials. I'm not talking about *writing* credentials, but a Ph.D. or M.D. degree. Books that deal with psychology or health stand a much better chance of selling if authored by someone who can legitimately be addressed as "Doctor." However, if you lack that distinction you can overcome the problem by coauthoring your book with someone possessing the proper academic or medical title.

How-to books also do well in the marketplace. These tell you how to buy, build, or sell a house; how to save money on car expenses, groceries, vacations, or clothes; how to ski, climb mountains, or scuba dive—in short, they provide instruction in every conceivable art, trade, or recreational pastime. As a rule, you won't need a graduate degree to author these books. Practical experience constitutes the only credentials needed here.

Regardless of the type of nonfiction book you elect to write, you can't let your own enthusiasm for the project outweigh practical considerations, namely: What is the likelihood of finding ten, twenty, thirty thousand, or more readers willing to plunk down the retail price of the book? How many people out there are actually going to be interested enough in what you say to buy your book? This is one of the big questions the editor you submit the book idea to is going to ask; it's one you'd better be ready to answer. How did you arrive at your probable readership figure? Was it a wild guess, or did some thought and research contribute to the conclusion? Have you talked to other authors in the field to find how well their books are selling? Do your magazine editors have any feel for the market? How closely can you pinpoint the audience you'll be trying to reach? These are basic marketing considerations you need to consider before attempting to sell your book, or even writing a proposal.

Another early step that shouldn't be overlooked is determining how many similar books are on the market. Check the current *Books In Print* at your local library to see if your chosen subject area is already overworked. The "Subject Guide" volumes are the easiest to use for this purpose and will let you quickly determine the amount of competition your book will face. If you find several dozen books covering the same general subject and note that at least a couple are titles appearing in the last few years, you may be better off forgetting the whole thing and starting over. However, if none of the titles suggests the same slant you intend to employ, it might be wise to proceed with your proposal. A lengthy title list also suggests healthy reader interest and if your book sheds new light on the subject or tackles it from a different angle, it may be a winner.

While you're doing this preliminary research, note which publishing houses seem most interested in your general subject area. *Books in Print* will tell you who's publishing the most titles about dog training, cheesemaking, or whatever, and *Writer's Market* or *Literary Market Place* will also give you a fair idea of the types of books a publisher is most interested in. There's no point wasting time sending your proposal to an inappropriate market.

The number of active book publishers in this country probably exceeds a thousand; the range from industry giants who publish several hundred new titles each year to small, specialized houses with a handful of annual offerings. Because the competition is terrific at "name" publishers like Doubleday and McGraw-Hill, you might be wise to send your first book proposal to one of the smaller companies, where it's apt to receive more personal attention. The big houses do buy from beginning authors, but you'll be bucking some heavy odds. You should check the *Writer's Market* listing to discover the name of the editor your book idea should be sent to. Large publishing houses may have several acquisition editors, each specializing in a different type of book. If you have trouble finding the right editor's name, telephone the publisher and ask.

Once you have both a subject and publisher in mind, it's time to start working up a proposal. Some writers simply go ahead and write the book, then submit the completed manuscript. This procedure may be advisable for first novelists, and if you've already written a book-length nonfiction manuscript you may as well package the whole thing and send it off. However, writing a nonfiction book without getting a contract or some commitment in advance is a bad gamble, and is something few professionals would even consider. This is where the proposal comes in.

A nonfiction book proposal consists of a cover letter introducing your idea and explaining why you think the book would sell, an in-depth outline, and one or two sample chapters. The cover letter is basically a sales tool. In it, you should explain how your book will differ from similar books already in print, how wide an audience the book will appeal to, your qualifications to author the book, and how large (word count) you think the book should be. An attention-getting title is also important. Because publishing is a profit-oriented business, any data or information you can present that will help convince the editor your book will sell, and sell well, should certainly be included. If you have any particular marketing ideas, this is the place to present them.

Many beginning authors ignore the question of salability when querying an editor—a serious mistake. That's the single thing the editor is most interested in, and if you fail to convince her that your book has real market potential you're guaranteed a negative reply. It should take only a few lines to tell her what your book is about and why you're qualified to write it. The rest of the cover letter should sell, sell, sell. If you can convince both the editor and her publisher boss that there are thousands of eager buyers just waiting for your book to show up on bookstore shelves, you can almost surely look forward to receiving a contract offer.

Don't make your cover letter too long. If you have a lot of hard-selling information that could help your chances of success, it's probably okay to let the query run into two pages—but no longer! A single page is better yet.

If you've had a number of articles published that relate to your book idea, you might mention the fact, along with the names of the periodicals they appeared in. If you've had a lot of practical experience that's pertinent, or if you've had academic training that would be helpful in writing the book, this should also be highlighted. A brief, separate résumé might even be a good idea if you can marshal an impressive amount of experience and accomplishments directly related to your proposal. On the other hand, there's no need to emphasize a lack of such credentials—your proposal should carry a positive tone throughout.

The outline you include with your proposal should list your chapter headings in the order they will appear in the book. Each chapter should be briefly summarized in turn. One or two well-written sample chapters complete the proposal package. Which chapters should you send? I find that the first, or introductory, chapter is often the most logical choice. This gives you a chance to show the editor how you intend to capture the reader's interest on that all-important first page. The first chapter also sets the book's tone and helps the editor determine its general thrust.

Once you've had a book or two published, you'll probably be able to sell future ideas on the strength of the proposal just described. If the cover letter and outline are adequate, a single sample chapter should do the trick, as long as it's representative of the rest of the book. However, most editors want to see more copy from an author who has yet to have his name printed on a dust jacket. I'd recommend sending at least two sample chapters when you're first starting out. The editor will probably ask to see more than a single chapter anyhow, so including a larger sample only saves you time.

Another way a freelancer can save time is to carefully photocopy the finished proposal and submit it to several publishing houses simultaneously. An original sales letter should go with each submission, carefully typed and addressed to the appropriate editor. Many book publishers don't care for multiple submissions, but you're under no obligation to indicate that your proposal is being sent to other editors. If you send your idea to one editor at a time and wait for his reply before resubmitting elsewhere, you'll be lucky to show it to six publishing houses in a year. It's only good business to accelerate the sales process. (Don't try multiple simultaneous submissions to competing magazines—that's a no-no.)

The entire proposal should be neatly typed, and mailed flat. Don't staple the pages together—use paper clips. There are special rates available for book manuscripts, but taking advantage of them isn't worth the few cents saved. In the first place, book-rate postage assures you a long delay before your material reaches an editor's office. Time is money to the free-lancer, and I can't imagine anyone who's spent the effort necessary to assemble a professional book proposal sending that material any way other than first class. First-class mail also receives more careful treatment en route, and is less likely to turn up missing. It makes a better impression on editors, too. Anything mailed second or third class arrives with a low-priority stigma, and doesn't say much for the writer's self-image. Don't forget to include a self-addressed return envelope with adequate postage affixed. This may sound like negative thinking, but most books sold go out two, three, or more times before a contract is issued. The odds are against your selling your idea to the first editor who sees it. If you don't include return postage in the form of a stamped, self-addressed envelope (SASE), you may have to type the whole thing over from your carbons—assuming you do make carbon copies of *everything* you mail. If you've been skipping this vital step, now's the time to mend your ways. Photocopies are even better if you have access to a machine and don't mind the few cents per copy expense.

What about an agent? The truth is, it's difficult for a brand-new author to acquire a good agent. By "good," I mean a respected professional who knows her job and works strictly on a 10-percent commission. There are a number of "agents" who advertise their willingness to "evaluate" your manuscript for a reading fee. As a rule, sending your material to such literary aid stations is an expensive waste of time. Agents who advertise may have some success in placing manuscripts with publishers, but they lack the high professional standing the nonadvertising authors' representatives hold in the eyes of publishers. The fact that you're paying a fee whether or not the book even sells somehow gives these "agents" a different perspective. The real pro collects nothing until the author's first advance is received. That's one of the reasons it's so tough for an untried author to find a reputable agent to represent him. The writer may or may not produce something salable, and an agent simply can't afford to spend a lot of time peddling a product that may never turn a profit for anyone.

Once you've successfully sold a book or two, you should have little trouble finding an agent. A list of professional authors' representatives appears in *Writer's Market*, or you can write the Society of Authors' Representatives, 101 Park Avenue, New York NY 10017 for a list of members. An agent can be a big help in getting your book proposal to the right people and is a *must* for negotiating movie rights, but don't look for this kind of assistance your first time out. The only exception to this rule might be an author who is a well-known sports or entertainment personality, or a prominent politician (or politician's secretary) with some scandal to divulge.

A beginning writer may be tempted to "submit" his work to one of the vanity publishers. These are subsidy publishers who contract to print and bind your book for a fee that runs into the thousands of dollars. In spite of blandishments to the contrary, that's *all* they do. Some kind of an advertising, promotion, and distribution program is usually implied but should be discounted from the beginning. Most bookstores refuse to stock books bearing a subsidy press imprint, and your chances of breaking even on the project, much less seeing future profit, are dismal indeed. If you hope to become a writing professional, subsidy publishing is a poor way to get started. The ads you see in the newspaper classified section soliciting "authors with books in progress" are vanity press come-ons. Ignore them.

Once you've mailed your proposal to a publisher, mark the date on your calendar and try to forget about it for the next sixty days. If you haven't received a reply by then, send a polite follow-up note inquiring about its status. Book editors are busy people, and the decision to offer a contract to a writer usually comes only after numerous staff meetings and evaluation sessions. At the same time, busy people sometimes fall into the habit of ignoring anything other than top-priority work until nudged into action. So if you don't hear anything for a couple of months, by all means get your "nudge" in the mail.

If your proposal comes back with a "no thanks" note attached, don't waste time mourning. Instead, write a new cover letter addressed to the next publisher on your list, and get the package out in the next mail.

If, on the other hand, your project finds a home and a contract is forthcoming, you have something to celebrate. But don't let your elation get out of hand until you've carefully read the offered contract. Better yet, pay an attorney to read it, too. Any legal contract is apt to contain a few pitfalls that are best avoided: it should be studied with care before you sign. Remember, contracts can be changed with line-outs and additions. If both parties agree to the changes made, all they have to do is initial each alteration. The contract needn't be rewritten in its entirety unless the number of changes required makes it unwieldy.

Most publishing houses have a basic, minimum contract. This usually includes a relatively low advance and a royalty schedule setting the terms of subsequent payments. In spite of what the editors tell you, virtually all contract terms are negotiable. However, as a brand-new author you're unfortunately vulnerable. You're not in any position to make too many demands until you've proven your worth in the marketplace. At the same time, it's best to pass up a deal too obviously stacked in the publisher's favor. The best bet here is to compare notes with other published authors as to what may or may not be fair, and rely heavily on your attorney's advice. When you finally get an agent, she can help you negotiate the best possible contract. Until then, you're pretty much on your own.

If you're offered a contract, you can sometimes use it as an enticement to acquire an agent. Ask him to represent you in the negotiations, and he may do just that. He earns a 10-percent commission without his usual amount of trouble and time, and that should put you on his list of clients. In addition, he'll see to it that the publisher doesn't take undue advantage.

The contract will stipulate a deadline that may be anywhere from four months to a year away. Once you agree to that deadline, do everything possible to see that your finished manuscript arrives on time. Since punctuality and dependability are highly cherished in the publishing world, if you earn a reputation for meeting deadlines you'll find it increasingly easier to land future contracts. Conversely, a reputation for chronic tardiness can do you real harm.

When writing a first novel, you may want to send the completed manuscript rather than try your luck with a partial and outline. In fact, most publishers insist on seeing the full manuscript before seriously considering a first novelist's work. If you've published numerous magazine articles or some nonfiction books, you might be able to get away with sending only a synopsis and a few sample chapters. Otherwise, you'll be better off mailing the entire book.

Again, it's important to send your fiction to the right publisher. Some houses specialize in westerns or mysteries to the exclusion of other genres, while others publish science fiction or historical romances. A mismatch wastes time and postage, so do your homework before putting your manuscript in the mail. A hard-selling cover letter isn't needed for most novels, as the publisher already has a good grasp of her market. If your novel resulted from some personal experience or was inspired by your five-year residency in a Tibetan monastery, you can transmit this information through the letter. Otherwise, keep it brief. Simply ask that your submission be considered, and let the manuscript speak for itself. Again, don't forget to include a separate envelope with return postage attached.

Writing a book seems an arduous task to the uninitiated. While it's a decidedly different experience than you face when beginning a magazine assignment, once you've completed that first book-length manuscript you'll discover it wasn't all that tough a chore. The second book comes considerably easier, and the third is easier yet. So make up your mind to start that first book *now*. Don't put it off. Start thinking tonight about a subject and title, and begin your proposal before the week is out. Procrastination is the writer's biggest enemy. If you hope to become a freelance success some day, the time to start realizing those goals isn't next month, next year, or five years down the road. If you ever hope to write a book, don't put if off. The ideal time to start is today.

10

Becoming a Full-Time Freelancer: When (If Ever) to Make the Break

After you've been writing and selling steadily on a part-time basis, it should soon become evident that your dollars-per-hour return from freelancing is considerably greater than what you earn from your regular job. Thus starts the dream of "someday" becoming a full-time writer.

The dream remains just that for most freelancers, since the majority of part-time writers never talk themselves into giving up the security of a nine-to-five situation. Of the handful who do work up courage to plunge into all-or-nothing self-employment, a high percentage find their dream turning into an economic nightmare before the first year is over.

The fact is, there's a high attrition rate among part-time freelancers who make the break from corporate employment to full-time freelancing. Their hopes go sour shortly after they leave their jobs, and many are forced to return to the company fold within months. Few stick it out past the first two years—but those who do have an excellent chance of succeeding in their newfound careers.

It's not poor writing skills that defeat so many full-time freelancers, but lack of economic preparedness. Once you're used to the security of a weekly or monthly paycheck, it's difficult to accept the catch-as-catch-can irregularity of free-lancing pay. Magazine checks show up in your mailbox at odd, unpredictable intervals, and your bank balance can fluc-tuate wildly. Even long-time professionals have lean periods. During my first few years of self-employment, my monthly income varied from $500 to an occasional high of $8,000 or more. It's difficult to plan a classic budget around that kind of cash flow, and if you're unable to salt extra funds away during the fat months, those lean months can become very lean indeed.

What's more, there are many hidden expenses the self-employed writer must contend with. These alone are enough to scuttle the dream if the freelancer hasn't had the foresight to plan ahead and include these expenses in her budget. What expenses? For starters, you'll need some kind of health-care plan for your family, if you have one, and hospitalization insurance becomes mighty expensive when you can't take advantage of group rates and the matching-fund discounts employers can offer. This is one area I had failed to investi-gate adequately, and I was shocked at how high the pre-miums were for full family coverage. As a result, I sweated through the first year without health-care insurance, and was fortunate my family didn't need it during that time. Two months after I finally enrolled in a plan, my son broke his ankle. The resulting hospital and doctor bills weren't over-whelming, but they would have put a substantial nick in my bill-paying budget without the financial backup my insur-ance provided. If we'd had to contend with a more serious injury or extended illness, the costs could have bankrupted us. Health-care insurance is something no full-time free-lancer can afford to be without, and if you can't afford the sky-high premiums you'll pay as a self-employed individual you can't afford to quit your regular job. So be sure to investi-gate such plans—and their costs—before you sever ties with your old job. If you're married and your spouse works, insur-ance can be carried through that employer.

When you *do* make the break, it's wise to enroll in the new plan early enough to insure continuous coverage through the transition period. Otherwise, there may be several weeks immediately following your self-employed status when you won't be protected by either plan. An injury or some other health problem occurring at that time could seriously jeopardize your freelancing plans.

Many companies offer low-cost life insurance to their employees as an added fringe benefit, and you may want to make up for lack of such coverage by buying a policy of similar value, particularly if your earnings are your family's sole income. Your writing may prove to be immortal, but you won't. So add those life-insurance premiums to that new budget.

Another consideration is office expenses. Although I had been writing from my den at home, I soon found there were too many interruptions to allow me to produce on a full-time schedule, and my wife had become accustomed to having the house empty each day while I was at work and the children were in school. This created some real adjustment problems, and by the end of my first month of freelancing full-time it became apparent I would have to rent an office. My experience is not unique, and I know other writers who work and live in separate locations. Freelancing requires a high degree of discipline and intense concentration, and a home writing environment is usually less than ideal for this work. In other words, you may have to add office rental to your monthly costs.

Other financial considerations include the lack of paid vacations. If you take two weeks off from your freelancing career, the money doesn't keep coming in. You earn every nickel you make, and when you stop writing your cash flow quickly evaporates. In other words, you must compensate for any time you take off by working longer and harder before and after your vacations.

Unless you intend to sit behind your typewriter until the undertaker lays you out, you'll need some income to retire on. Again, this is a fringe benefit you'll have to provide without company help. You may or may not be able to count on any aid from Social Security by the time you turn sixty-five (if you're younger than fifty now, there's a good chance all that money will be spent by the time you're ready to collect), so you'd better plan on squirreling away a substantial sum each year to keep you off welfare when you're too old to type.

Don't forget to budget for increased telephone expenses and such incidentals as photo processing costs. Some magazine writers spend upwards of $200 a month having film developed and black-and-white prints made to submit with their manuscripts, and that cuts deeply into the gross income.

The point I'm trying to make is that while you'll probably increase your writing income when you turn to freelancing full-time, your expenses are likely to take a jump, too. You'll be able to save in some areas—your new working clothes can consist of shorts and sandals or jeans and cowboy boots rather than business dress—but other costs will certainly go up. A very conservative writing-office budget, with $100 going toward rent, $100 allotted for phone calls, and $25 for paper, postage, and paper clips will chomp $225 from your monthly income. Figure another $100 or so for the hospitalization insurance included as a fringe in your old job, and maybe $50 for life insurance, and you're looking at $375 that has to come off the top before you can buy groceries or pay off the mortgage. You'll also have to set a chunk aside for federal and state income and self-employment taxes. Subtract the funds you withhold for your retirement, and your monthly net becomes smaller and smaller.

Such are the economic necessities of a full-time freelance career. The expenses I've mentioned are a simple fact of life; they're nothing more than normal business costs. They shouldn't faze you unless you failed to take them into consideration when laying your plans.

If I've painted a bleak picture up to this point, it's because many freelancers fail for lack of proper planning and foresight. Too often, they're blinded to economic fact by the romance and freedom they think freelancing offers, and when they discover that it's just another business they're shocked and disappointed. Those writers who enter this business with their eyes wide open have a much better chance of succeeding.

With that out of the way, let's take a look at when—if ever—

you should consider giving up your regular job to freelance full time. I've already pointed out that many successful part-time writers earn considerably more on an hourly basis for the time they spend freelancing than they do during their daytime jobs. When you discover that your efforts for two or three nights a week provide as much income as forty hours at the office, the seeds of discontent start to sprout.

At this point, several things usually prevent the part-time freelancer from giving his or her employer two weeks' notice. The first is that while the weekly or hourly freelance income may be substantially higher than that earned on the job, this after-hours money isn't steady enough to count on. You may have a great month with checks showing up every few days, but hear nothing at all from editors in the month that follows. Many full-time writers have the same problem, and the cautious freelancer recognizes the difficulties that can result from unstable cash flow.

Another common deterrent to switching from part-time to full-time freelancing when writing income rises is that people tend to live up to (or beyond) whatever income level is available. In other words, if you're earning $18,000 from your regular job and another $18,000 writing, it doesn't take long to discover that you absolutely can't live on less than $36,000 a year. If you allow yourself to fall into this particular trap, you may never feel you can afford to make the break.

Nonetheless, this is the usual breaking point. When freelancing income rises to equal or exceed the salary they make in their regular jobs, many writers feel confident enough in their earning power to become completely self-employed. This is especially true if the freelance income has been coming in steadily over several months, and is the result of considerably less time and effort than that expended at the office.

Even if the freelancer has been living fully up to both incomes, he may reason that by spending the extra time he'll have available when he quits his regular job, he'll be able to earn much more. That's the premise most freelancing careers are built around, and it sometimes works out that way. Unfortunately, doubling time spent at the typewriter doesn't guarantee doubling income.

One reason putting in more freelancing time may not result in an immediately increased income is that a writer needs to broaden his editorial contacts to add to his sales base. The editors you sold to so regularly while freelancing part-time may now be buying at their capacity. The fact that you have more time to write won't mean much to these people if they can't use more manuscripts. Thus you can't assume your market will automatically expand to accept your greater output.

Another problem some writers discover is that they lack sufficient discipline to sit behind a typewriter five or six hours at a time, day in and day out. While they were comfortable with a three-times-a-week, two-hours-at-a-time writing schedule squeezed in after the working day, they just can't function for longer, uninterrupted stretches on a daily basis.

Other writers find they miss the companionship of office workers. Writing can be a lonely profession. Spending days on end in the exclusive company of your typewriter can give you an insular outlook on life. If you're basically a social person, the adjustment can be severe.

Now that I've trotted out the negative and cautionary points, let me admit that full-time freelancing can be a highly rewarding experience and is well worth working toward. Being your own boss carries risks whether you're a freelance writer, building contractor, or baker. If your business fails, you can blame no one but yourself. On the other hand, there's a lot of personal satisfaction gained from meeting those risks head on and succeeding. Deep down, most creative types find it tough accepting corporate higher authority and generally have enough maverick in them to yearn for the freedom a freelancer enjoys.

For one thing, it's nice to set your own working hours. Some people are basically night people and function better after the sun goes down; others do their finest work in the early part of the day. A freelancer can begin her writing sessions at 2:00 a.m. if she wants to, since there's no clock to punch in this business.

While in freelancing there's not the conventional security a corporate employee enjoys, the freelancer claims an entirely different type of security. He's not tied to the fortunes of a single company, and the continuance of his income doesn't depend on keeping one or two supervisors happy. Instead, his work is divided among several clients, and this spreads economic risk. If one publisher is forced into bankruptcy or if you rub an editor the wrong way, there are always other publishers and editors to fall back on. This means you don't have to worry about being fired or laid off because your employer is suffering economic ills.

Another advantage is the freelancer's ability to set his own income level. Instead of being limited to a 5- to 10-percent annual salary increase, a writer can double or even triple his income in a single year. On the other hand, your annual earnings can also drop. Whether your fortunes rise or fall is entirely up to you and your writing and business abilities.

The intelligent thing to do before making the radical change in lifestyle that full-time freelancing requires is to carefully weigh the advantages and disadvantages of self-employment. Some people are temperamentally well-suited to the freelancing life, others are not. There are risks involved, and if you're the head of a household with heavy monthly expenses, you should certainly be more cautious about making a major employment change than a single person with fewer responsibilities has to be. However, I turned to full-time freelancing with a wife, three sons, and a cat to support. And while the first year was scary enough for my wife to seriously consider finding a paying job, we never had to fall back on that contingency.

If you're married, be sure to talk things over with your spouse. You'll need his or her wholehearted support in the months ahead, and unless you're in accord from the beginning, matters can get rocky indeed. The paychecks will almost surely be sporadic at first, and you'll have to budget carefully until your income stabilizes—if, in fact, it ever does. If your spouse is employed, this can considerably ease the strain. This is especially true if you can scale down your spending to make do on that single income if necessary; you can also purchase health insurance through your spouse's company policy.

It's possible to go it alone, but if your income is your family's only support there are important precautions to take. The first is to cut down spending on credit a full year in advance of your anticipated liberation. This implies careful planning, which rules out any spur-of-the-moment changes in your employment situation. It's important to reduce your monthly bills to a manageable sum, as there will be months when few, if any, checks arrive in the afternoon mail.

You should gradually step up your part-time writing efforts several months before quitting your job. This helps you adjust to the idea of producing more work and gives you a chance to broaden your sales base. Contact new editors during this period, while at the same time solidifying your relationship with those who already buy from you regularly. It won't hurt to let editors you've been selling to know of your plans, and see if you can get some commitment from them to buy more of your work in the future.

Your increased activity should give you a little extra cash to work with. While much of this should go into savings, it's prudent to get two or three months ahead in your mortgage payments as a possible buffer for those periods when little money comes in. Prepaying a car payment or so is an excellent idea, as it gives you a bit of breathing room and also bolsters your credit rating. If you've had any credit problems in the past, this is the time to take care of them. A good credit history can be an invaluable asset to anyone who's thinking of becoming self-employed. Cross your fingers you won't need to borrow money in the months ahead, but if it becomes necessary you'll be able to qualify for a loan.

Ideally, you should have a full six months' income tucked away in a savings account before you quit regular employment to freelance full-time. With that kind of cash in reserve and your monthly bills reduced, you should be in pretty good shape to begin your freelance career. People have turned to self-employment with less ready money on hand, but this adds to the risk of failure. Chapter 13 deals with juggling finances if you get into cash-flow difficulties, but the best bet is to have extra funds available from the beginning.

When should you make the break to full-time freelancing?

When you reach the point where your part-time earnings from magazine and book writing equal or exceed your salary from that nine-to-five job—and not just once, but for several months running—it's realistic to start planning the break. This means retiring the credit cards, paying off as many bills as possible, and working toward having a full six months' income drawing interest in a savings account.

Editors who learn of your plans to freelance full-time may offer well-meaning advice like, "You're crazy to quit that company you've been working for all these years," or "Full-time freelancing? Don't do it!" They've seen too many others follow the same route you're contemplating, and if they try to talk you out of it it's only because they feel they're doing you a favor. And remember, they could be right. But be reassured that most writers who've tried and failed at full-time free-lancing did so because they weren't financially prepared and didn't know what to expect. Forewarned is forearmed, and that's one reason I've outlined so many drawbacks to our precarious trade.

Cut down on your usual spending (you'll probably have to anyhow to build up your savings) and do everything you can to bring expenses into line. Instead of going to an expensive restaurant, buy a couple of steaks at the supermarket and have dinner at home. At today's prices, steaks are a luxury, too, but your meal will be a whole lot cheaper if you prepare it yourself. If possible, pay off bills early. This will reduce your total debt load, while at the same time building your credit rating. And don't forget to get a few months ahead on the mortgage and car payments.

It wouldn't hurt to stock the larder with canned goods bought in case-lot sales. (You'll save money, and will be able to eat *something* if those lean months fall back to back.) You'd also be wise to start buying clothes at the end of the season when they're on sale, rather than a month or so earlier at full retail price. In short, try living the life of a cheapskate. If pinching pennies becomes too repugnant, you may not be cut out for the life of a full-time freelancer. If you're fortunate you'll soon once more stock your wardrobe with clothes in season and eat in fancy restaurants, but for now the word is *economize*. At least get used to the idea of low-budget living, as there's an excellent chance you'll be exposed to this lifestyle, however briefly, when you become self-employed.

As your target date approaches, talk things over once again with your spouse. Make sure you're in full agreement on that big step ahead and that you both know what you may be letting yourselves in for. If you're lucky you'll be earning more money than ever in a year or two, but there are no guarantees. Recognize the risk involved, and plan to minimize its possible effect.

When you feel fully prepared emotionally and financially to leave the security of your job, make sure you have the necessary insurance coverage (both medical and life). Have your typewriter overhauled to meet the heavy needs of the months ahead (if its life expectancy seems doubtful, buy a new one and keep the old as a spare), stock up on ribbons, paper, and supplies, take a deep breath, and go have that talk with your boss.

A word of caution here—don't, whatever you do, burn any bridges with your former employer. Explain to her your desire to freelance, and try to leave the door open for possible reemployment at some future date if it should prove necessary. This only makes sense, as any business enterprise can fail for a variety of reasons, and a self-employed writer may find himself ready for the corporate life once again before the first year is out. Hope this won't be the case, but meanwhile, it doesn't hurt to leave your old job in such a way that your ex-employer has good feelings toward you. If you've been working as a copywriter or in some related capacity, you might even suggest doing some of this work on a freelance basis once you leave.

If I haven't managed to talk you out of the notion by now, you may indeed have what it takes to make a go of full-time freelancing. You'll be entering an exclusive club whose numbers are few, and both risks and rewards are great. If you're prepared to survive the first full year of writing for your living, you should know by then whether the freelancing life is for you. For those who try and succeed, an enviable lifestyle awaits.

11

Time Is Money: Business Realities of the Full-Time Writer

When you turn to freelancing on a full-time basis, you quickly develop a new attitude toward the business. Checks once received as a welcome adjunct to regular corporate pay suddenly become a subject of overriding interest. Editors who refuse to pay decent rates are dropped from consideration; magazines with strict pay-on-publication (POP) policies are no longer queried for assignments.

You soon find yourself figuring out ways to save time or squeeze more hours into every working day. Manuscripts once painstakingly honed through multiple editing sessions now go through the typewriter no more than twice—and sometimes the first draft is mailed when a deadline is imminent. This means you have to tighten up those writing skills and do everything better first time around. If you hope for a decent yearly income, you can't afford to spend several days writing a piece that's going to earn just $200. You must cultivate speed and accuracy when assembling a manuscript, and learn to judge closely beforehand how much time and energy an assignment will require.

As a freelance writer, you're a businessman with a single

commodity at your disposal: time. Every hour you spend on a writing project must net an acceptable return on that precious investment, or you'll eventually find yourself out of business. The old saw, "Time is money," takes on new meaning as you turn your energies toward freelancing fulltime.

How much is your time worth? That's a question only you can answer—but don't let some editor make the decision for you. If you've decided you must gross at least $20 for each hour spent on a writing assignment, don't be talked into accepting a lesser fee. Remember to include both research and writing time when estimating what an article should pay. It's difficult to make a decent living writing $100 articles, but there are some such "pin money" assignments that take only an hour or two to turn out. At the same time, there are magazines that typically pay $800 to $1000 or more for full-length features, but many of these assignments are ultimately less profitable than the $100 quickies because they demand so much more time and effort.

The trick is to establish the proper balance in the assignments you seek and accept. In my experience, it's difficult to make an adequate living writing exclusively either massproduced but low-paying pieces or the $1000-and-up assignments offered by more prestigious periodicals. To earn $40,000 a year turning out $75 to $100 manuscripts, you'll have to write between 400 and 500 such pieces. If you figure time off for an occasional collapse due to fatigue, that works out to around two articles a day. Maintain that pace very long (assuming you can find enough low-paying assignments you can complete on such a schedule) and you'll be an excellent candidate for confinement in a rubber room.

If you go the prestige market route, you might be able to earn the same yearly amount writing just thirty or thirty-five pieces. Fewer than three articles a month sounds like a leisurely pace, but merely obtaining that many guaranteedpay assignments from better-known magazines could prove as difficult in the long run as cranking out a pair of cheaper pieces each day. Competition is heavy at the top, and pegging your expectations to this market exclusively is risky, indeed.

A more reasonable approach is to follow the middle ground. There are many magazines that pay in the $300 to $600 range for competently written pieces; writing one hundred or so such manuscripts annually should put you in a comfortable earnings bracket. These "middle magazines" are much easier to sell to than the top-paying publications, but even a hundred articles a year is a heavy load. A few years back I wrote and sold 138 separate pieces during a twelve-month period, and the experience left me thoroughly drained, both physically and emotionally. Some of those sales were columns 300 or 400 words long which took only an hour or two to write, but the majority were 1,500- to 2000-word features. When you must produce in such volume, writing becomes progressively less fun. And if you're not enjoying what you're doing, you'd better start making other plans regardless of the earnings your efforts bring in.

A frenetic writing pace has other dangers, too. Overexposure to the typewriter can bring on a monumental case of writer's block, and it's even possible to suffer a physical breakdown under the continuing strain of day-in, day-out composition. I hardly need mention the mental and emotional problems such a lifestyle is likely to produce. At best, writers tend to suffer alternate bouts of mania and depression, but when you're under the unremitting strain of late deadlines compounded by occasional cash-flow problems, your family will be hard pressed to cope with you and your troubles.

The trick is to diversify, to try to line up exactly the right number of short-and-easy and long-and-hard assignments to space out over the year. A typical month's combination might be a regular column or two each month for magazines with which you have a long-standing relationship, maybe two or three medium-pay articles in the $300 to $500 range, and a more lucrative feature for one of the higher-paying magazines. If you can then arrange to work on one or possibly two books each year, and sandwich this writing in to take up any slack between magazine assignments, you should be able to profitably use any and all available time without allowing too much pressure to build. Most nonfiction book contracts call for a delivery date six months to a year from the day the agreement is signed. If you start work on the manuscript within the first few weeks and set a timetable of X number of chapters to be completed each month, you'll be able to put together an 80,000-word book with no real strain on your magazine schedule. At the same time, you won't have to worry about unproductive gaps between assignments: If you have nothing else scheduled for the day, you can always turn out a few more pages of your latest book.

Every writer comes up with her own feature—column—book mix because each freelancer has different skills and needs. Even book assignments vary greatly. Novels may add blessed variety to a magazine writer's nonfiction schedule; some free-lancers have fiction and nonfiction books in the works simultaneously. Each requires its own discipline, and switching back and forth often proves as refreshing as avoiding the typewriter entirely. Because novels—particularly first novels—are difficult to presell on the basis of an outline and proposal, it's wise to spend part of your book-writing time on nonfiction projects. Of course, you should never complete more than one or two sample chapters and an expanded outline of any nonfiction book without a written contract and cash advance. Writing books for which there may be no ready market is a gamble the full-time freelancer can't afford. Unless you've reached the enviable stage in your fiction-writing career where your novels can be sold on your past reputation, you should make nonfiction your number one priority. Once you've got a self-help or how-to book contract signed and another proposal or two under consideration, you can allow yourself the luxury of beginning a novel.

The above rule is a general one, merely a suggestion drawn from my own experience. Some authors flourish best when writing dialogue or plotting a novel's progress. If you're more at home writing fiction, by all means spend your energies as inclination dictates. However, you should put this kind of work in its proper perspective and recognize the time you spend at it for the gamble it is. It may pay off, and handsomely, but there's no guarantee that your fiction-writing efforts will be rewarded with cold, hard cash. And that's the stuff you need to buy groceries. Until you establish your reputation as a novelist, don't allow yourself to spend so much time on fiction that your bread-and-butter assignments suffer.

By the time you've sold a book or two, you'll start wondering about the services an author's representative, or agent, provides. A good agent can be a big help, not only in selling your manuscripts but in negotiating the best possible contract. She is supposed to know which publishers are in the market for which subjects, and have a reasonable idea of what a particular project should be worth. In addition, proposals submitted by an agent usually get faster consideration than over-the-transom packages sent in by the author himself. While you or I may wait two or three months for a reply, an agent will usually have an answer within thirty days.

Being represented by a professional gives you more credibility than most authors without agents enjoy; a publisher is more likely to take your proposal seriously if it has an agent's recommendation. However, no agent can work miracles, and an unsalable manuscript remains just that. Conversely, any really good book should eventually sell whether or not an agent enters the picture. The work or proposal must stand on its own merits in the end.

Many writers swear by their agents and wouldn't think of working without them. Others have become disenchanted with agents over the years, and now market their work independently. Still others have achieved considerable success on their own and have never seen reason to shave 10 percent from their gross income.

If you've written extensively in a particular field, you may have better contacts where it counts than any agent possibly could. The more specialized your expertise, the more likely you are to have such contacts. Most agents have their own favorite markets or specialties, and it is unrealistic to expect a literary agent to have intimate acquaintance with all fields of publishing. Some authors' representatives are particularly good with fiction and know exactly where to send your new historical romance. Others may be better acquainted with self-help publishing houses, or absolutely up on the latest trends in science fiction.

In short, selecting the right agent can be as critical as choosing the right publisher. There are good agents and bad agents, and some who are just average. There are also large establishments and small. If you're represented by a well-known New York agency with many famous clients, you may feel your work is shunted aside in favor of more glamorous authors. A smaller agency may give your efforts more personal attention, but you may, in turn, wonder about *their* overall effectiveness in finding the right publishers for your material.

Avoid those literary agencies that advertise and offer to evaluate your manuscripts for a "reader's fee." Legitimate authors' representatives work strictly on commission (10 percent has long been established as *the* rate agents charge; more is unacceptable), and generally agree to accept as clients only authors having a real shot at long-term success. Your first book or two may not make anyone—you, your agent, or your publisher—any money, but both agent and publisher will often wager on the possibility of your producing a genuine commercial success the second or third time around.

Most agents are interested in handling book-length properties only. It's not economically practicable for them to peddle magazine articles that may gross $600 or $800 (or less)—their cut is too small to compensate for the effort. There are exceptions, but magazine assignments are best handled through direct writer-editor contact.

I've had mixed experience with literary agents, and know other writers who alternately praise and curse their own representatives. When an agent places your proposal quickly and comes up with a fat advance and an otherwise favorable contract, he's a hero. But when he shops your work around to several publishers without success, his brightness dims. My own agent recently tried unsuccessfully to place a proposal of mine that he had at first been particularly enthusiastic about. After sending it off to more than a half-dozen publishers, he finally returned it to me with his regrets. I promptly mailed it to the publisher I first had in mind when I prepared the proposal, and it sold immediately! Why my agent ignored that publisher is a mystery to me, since the publisher in question seemed to be the most logical firm to approach from the beginning. The book I'm talking about is the one you're reading now.

All this goes to show that agents—like editors, writers, and publishers—are merely human and can err in judgment from time to time. So if and when you do find one to represent you, don't accept her judgment as the final word. Have faith in your work, and if your agent gives up keep submitting it on your own. Perseverance plays a big part in freelancing success, as does confidence in your own ideas and abilities.

Ideally, you'll develop a comfortable working relationship with your agent and the association will prove mutually profitable. However, author-agent marriages sometimes end on the rocks, and there are writers who switch agents with the same frequency some Hollywood types change spouses and paramours. Some successful authors, once agented, are now going it alone. Others market their own work but retain an attorney to negotiate contracts.

While you may not be interested in having a lawyer do your bargaining, any writer would do well to seek legal advice before signing any publishing agreement. If possible, locate an attorney with prior experience in publishing and trust his advice. Since most contracts are issued by the publisher, it stands to reason such agreements will be slanted in his favor. All publishing contracts are negotiable to a degree, and your attorney should be able to advise you of any changes that should be made.* (See chapter 12.)

Of course, if you've yet to have that first book published, the question of agents is largely academic. You *might* be able to convince a reputable agent to represent you without a proven track record to back you up, but you'd be better off

---

*The Authors Guild, Inc., 234 West 44th Street, New York, NY 10036 makes a standard book contract form available to members; this can be compared to any publishing contracts offered. Another excellent guide to contracts is *A Writer's Guide to Book Publishing*, by Richard Balkin, Hawthorn Books, Inc., 260 Madison Ave., New York, NY 10016.

spending the energy selling that first proposal to a publisher. *Then* you can start thinking about finding an agent.

While books and agents become increasingly important as your freelance career grows, chances are the bulk of your income for several years will be derived from magazine writing. Thus, the business of separating the potentially profitable assignments from the unprofitable ones assumes increasing importance.

One of the first things you should do upon becoming a full-time freelancer is to weed out your "low pay—slow pay" editors. Magazines that can't pay you enough to realize your determined minimum hourly rate should be eased from your query list. It's possible once-recalcitrant editors might have a change of heart regarding pay scales when they learn you really mean business, but don't count on it. You'll *have to* upgrade your markets and please editors who may be more persnickety. Any time you raise your sights in the publishing business, the competition automatically becomes stiffer. However, the step from $200-an-article markets to magazines paying twice as much is hardly a giant one. In fact, this is a step you should have taken while you were still freelancing part-time. If you overlooked it, now's the time to take care of it.

Low pay is one thing; slow pay is something else again. There are a number of fairly well-paying magazines that continue to insist on payment on—or after—publication. I vented my spleen on such publishers in chapter 6, so let me only reiterate that such POP arrangements are highly precarious for the writer and should be avoided. I know from experience it's possible to be dead broke with $6,000 or $7,000 on the books owed by POP publications. Such magazines are working on your money—interest-free—while you're forced to take out a costly bank loan to cover day-to-day expenses.

Suffice it to say that few successful full-time freelancers deal with POP magazines—that is, unless the publisher makes an under-the-counter exception to keep the writer in his stable. You'll have enough trouble with cash flow during that important first year without the added problems "low pay—slow pay" editors can give you.

How do you decide when to "fire" an editor? The answer is simple—when you're getting enough better-paying assignments to keep you busy, and you're beginning to feel overworked. If the editor in question can't—or won't—raise his pay scale to the higher level, it's time to move on. There's no need to alienate the editor, or even to give him official notice you're moving to higher-paying markets. When you quit querying him for new assignments or start to turn down proffered ones, he'll soon get the message. It doesn't pay to burn any bridges. Your more lucrative markets may one day dry up, or an editor you've angered in the past may suddenly show up at the helm of a more prestigious publication. Memories can be long in this business, and enemies are never an asset to a freelance career.

In the previous chapter I mentioned the possible need for an office away from home. This obviously increases your monthly expenses, since rent and commuting costs must be added to the burden. Is it worth it? You're the only one who can answer that question. If you have an office or den in your home that's sufficiently isolated to let you concentrate on writing five or six hours each and every day, you may not need a separate office. But remember—each of those interruptions destroys your concentration and thus costs you money. If your time is worth twenty-five or thirty dollars an hour, you don't have to lose much of that precious commodity to pay the rent on a remote office. If leasing an office increases your productivity, it's money well spent. At home, there's always the temptation to go to the fridge for a snack, watch daytime soap operas (which may do irreparable harm to your creative abilities and anesthetize the brain), or make romantic advances to your spouse—anything but face that unresponsive keyboard. A sparsely equipped office offers fewer distractions. Once you've sharpened all the pencils, rearranged the paper clips, and cleaned the typewriter keys, there's not much else to do. So you write.

The telephone is another potential time-robber, whether you write from a ten-by-ten-foot office downtown or from your walnut-paneled libary at home. Because freelancing can be such a lonely profession, many writers pick up the phone at the slightest provocation. Long-distance calls to editors or fellow freelancers can make your monthly Ma Bell greeting card frightening to behold, and time you spend chatting produces little in the way of cash return. So beware the telephone! Regard it as a necessary and potentially expensive evil, and keep your hands off the alluring instrument as much as possible.

The trick to making money in freelancing is to use your time effectively. Forget the ten o'clock coffee break, and set aside other reflexes learned in your corporate life. You're no longer on salary—wasted time costs you money. If you must eat lunch, make it a quick sandwich at the corner drugstore— or better yet, bring a snack from home. If you're already home, avoid turning the event into a twelve-course extravaganza that gobbles time and needless calories.

An enterprising freelancer can find endless ways to waste time. But if she's to succeed at her chosen profession, she'll quickly learn discipline.

Writing time isn't the only time you can waste. When you're working on an assignment involving travel, you can often parlay the trip into multiple-article coverage. Look for related features that can be sold to noncompeting magazines. Human-interest stories are available everywhere, and with practice you should have no difficulty gathering material for several features from a single assignment. This means knowing your markets and keeping in touch with a number of editors.

The technique of turning a single idea into three or four articles is one every professional writer quickly learns. It's all a matter of using different slants and treatments. Just be sure you market the spin-off pieces to noncompeting publications. Playing both ends against the middle can land you in trouble if the editor who gave you the original assignment sees similar features in magazines sharing the same readership.

Full-time freelancing is a demanding profession, but it can be a lucrative one, as well. To succeed at it, you must learn to earn more money with less effort. You set your own fees and earning potential; all you must do is stay on schedule.

12

Royalties: The Full-Time Freelancer's Best Friend

The biggest problem a full-time freelancer faces is generating sufficient funds to pay the monthly bills and deposit a little cash in savings or an investment account. Because inflation keeps nibbling away at our earning power and many magazines persist in paying rates lagging ten years (or more) behind the times, it becomes increasingly difficult for a writer to stay solvent.

Even if you're lucky enough to write for top-paying magazines, each check evaporates quickly under the pressure of consumer prices. Since you're paid only once for each authorial effort, you have to work harder each year simply to stay in the same economic standing, let alone get ahead. The rat race isn't limited to corporate commuter types; writers can find themselves running in the same narrow lane with the greyhound slowly closing on their heels. Once you reach the top of a magazine's pay scale, the only way you can make more money is to produce in greater volume and continually expand your markets.

If working harder and harder each year isn't your idea of an idyllic lifestyle, take heart. The freelance writer has something going that regular wage earners do not: royalties.

Book royalties are the writer's answer to economic enslavement, and may provide your only path to long-term security as a full-time freelancer. Unlike magazine checks that dry up immediately when you stop sending out manuscripts, the right book can keep on yielding income many years after the work is completed.

While this is what every author works for, many of the new titles appearing each year fail to spark sufficient sales to warrant reprinting; thus, future proceeds may never materialize. This is an unfortunate fact authors must keep in mind when developing book ideas. How long is interest in the subject likely to remain keen? It's also wise to work with a publisher who maintains a strong backlist of titles. Refer to the *Publisher's Trade List Annual* at your local bookstore or library to determine this.

The annual royalties from a single book may not be impressive, but the income thus generated can be built upon as other books appear under your byline. Book authors usually receive an earnings statement twice a year, along with a check for monies owed to date. Such checks may range from a few hundred to several thousand dollars, depending on how successfully the book is selling. What's more, there may be unexpected bonuses when a hardcover book is optioned by a paperback house, or when foreign rights are sold. If the book in question is a fast-selling novel, there's always the chance that some Hollywood producer will want to base a film upon it. Because of this possibility, the author should be careful not to sign away most of his motion-picture rights. (This is where a good agent comes in. The Author's Guild recommends that no more than 10 percent of such rights be retained by the publisher.)

The important thing about royalties and other such proceeds is that all occur well after the fact. When you publish a book you should hold out for a large enough advance to make writing the book economically feasible for that alone, and then any other money the book makes for you is pure gravy. The advance is paid back from royalties accumulated after the book is in print, and once that debt is retired you can look for some supplemental income, at least, in years ahead.

How much can a book earn in royalties? The amount can vary from zero to hundreds of thousands—even millions—of dollars. The return is affected by several factors. The first, of course, is the book's popularity in the marketplace: The more copies that sell, the more money you get. Longevity is another factor. Some books are marketed over a relatively short time, and have lifespans better measured in months than years. Fad books can sell wildly when first introduced, only to be remaindered before the year is out. The market for printed matter can be highly unpredictable, and timing is extremely important.

If possible, you should select a subject that isn't overly perishable. It would also be advantageous for your book to attract wide readership. A publisher's decision to print a book is no guarantee of its ultimate profitability. Some proposals are purchased in full knowledge that no more than a few thousand copies are likely to sell. If this is the case, the only money you'll ever see for your efforts will be the advance you agreed upon—yet another reason to get the initial ante as high as you can before signing that contract.

Another factor affecting a book's potential earning power is the negotiated royalty rate. A few publishers prefer to purchase manuscripts outright, which means the author receives nothing beyond the purchase price. The only way such an arrangement can be beneficial to a writer is if the price is high enough to compensate him adequately for his time. I have written two books under flat-purchase contracts. The first I completed in just a few weeks; it gave me a highly satisfactory dollars-per-hour return. I received a substantially higher price for my second such effort, but I badly miscalculated the length of time required to write the book. I was forced to do more research than anticipated, with the result that I actually may have *lost* money on the project, as I ended up turning down several more lucrative assignments in order to fulfill the book contract. Even so, I was still late.

As a general rule, I would advise against writing books on a flat-fee basis. Under such circumstances, the book becomes nothing more than an oversized magazine assignment, and you realize none of the later benefits from royalties or sales of other rights. It's usually far more advantageous from a writer's point of view to have some kind of royalties coming in.

Most books are sold to publishers today under royalty contracts. However, the terms of these contracts vary greatly, and the mere fact that you have a royalty agreement is no guarantee you have a *good* agreement. Royalty rates can vary from 5 to 6 percent (or less) for a paperback up to a high of 15 percent or more. Several different rates may be quoted in the contract for special promotion or book club sales, and to make things even more complicated a few publishers base the royalty rate on net rather than gross sales. Since the net is around 60 percent of the usual list, or retail price, a rate based on 10 percent of *net* sales actually amounts to 6 percent or less of the list price.

If there is any such thing as a standard contract (and there probably isn't), it would be one with royalties beginning at 10 percent of the book's retail price and escalating to 12½ and, finally, 15 percent as sales grow. A typical agreement might stipulate the 10-percent figure for the first 5,000 copies sold, 12½ percent for the next 5,000, and top out at 15 percent once sales reach the 10,000-book mark. However, each publisher has his own ideas about what constitutes the ideal contract, and these numbers (and percentages) can vary considerably.

All book contracts are negotiable to some degree, and this is where a good agent can earn his keep. Many writers find it more comfortable—and sometimes more profitable—to let their agents handle the financial battles. Your agent is probably more skilled in the give-and-take haggling book publishers expect, and he also has a pretty fair idea of what a given market is likely to bear. The fact that the agent stands to collect 10 percent of the negotiated price guarantees he has your interests at heart. If you work without an agent you'll simply have to rely on your own bargaining skills. The contract you ultimately agree upon depends on how badly the publisher wants your book, and how little you're willing to accept to write it. Remember that the contract the publisher first offers is merely the one he *hopes* you'll accept. It will be written to favor the publisher as much as possible, and the advance and royalty figures may both be open to negotiation.

Your bargaining position and skills will improve as you establish a publishing record. The first-time author is largely at the mercy of any publisher who offers her a contract, as the publisher has no way of knowing if she's capable of putting together a publishable book in the time requested. You're an unknown quantity, and the contract you'll be offered is likely to reflect this uncertainty. At the same time, you should never accept a contract that won't allow you a decent return on your time and energy.

I've seen publishing contracts in which the author's royalty was set at a certain cash figure rather than a percentage of sales price. While such a figure may seem perfectly acceptable when you sign the contract, this kind of agreement works to your disadvantage if the book continues in print for several years. Inflation affects book publishers as it does any other business, with the result that a book may bear a higher price tag each time it is reprinted. Thus a book that sold for $8.95 a few short years ago may fetch $11.95 or more in its later editions. If you agreed on a royalty of $1.35 a copy rather than 15 percent of the purchase price, you'll actually be earning less with each subsequent printing. The $1.35 figure remains the same, but is worth less as inflation erodes its buying power. Keeping royalties pegged to a percentage of the purchase price hedges against inflation and assures you an increasing return the longer the book stays in print.

Since most royalty rates are figured as a percentage of the list price, the book's price itself is another factor affecting your earnings. However, this is a factor beyond the author's control. The publisher's production people carefully study each book proposal before it's purchased, and a retail price is decided on that should encourage sales while allowing a reasonable per-unit profit. The publisher decides the book's price.

Obviously, the longer your book stays in print and available to bookstores, the more money you stand to make. Publishers have different criteria regarding a book's longevity, as well as different distribution and promotion policies. This means you should check a publisher's past performance before submitting your proposal. One way to do this is to refer to *Books in Print* for similar books issued by that publishing house. When were these books originally published? If none of the titles listed is more than a year or two old, it could be an indication of the company's willingness to quickly remainder a book once sales drop below a certain level. The publisher's current catalog (which you can send for) gives you the same information.

All things being equal, you should try to place your work with a publisher who's likely to keep it alive as long as possible. You may be better off accepting a contract with less favorable royalty figures from a publisher reputed to keep past titles in circulation than agreeing to slightly higher rates from a house that may drop your book from the market in the next year. Promotion is also important. If your publisher is willing to spend money advertising your book, you'll benefit through increased sales.

Another reliable indication of how well the publisher really expects your book to sell can be found in the size of the initial printing. This number may or may not be spelled out in your contract, but it can usually be learned simply by asking the editor assigned to work with you on the project. If only 2,000 or 3,000 copies are scheduled to be run it can be interpreted as a lack of faith in probable sales. At the very least it indicates caution on the publisher's part. Conversely, an initial printing of 10,000 or more shows a healthy optimism. The more copies printed, the heavier stake the publisher has in the book's success. This usually means your book will receive adequate promotion, and can be taken as an excellent sign that the book will do well financially.

Once your book is in print, you can contribute to its success by indulging in a little self-promotion. If the publisher dreams of seeing your book on the best-seller lists, he may arrange for you to appear on radio or television talk shows at his expense. By all means cooperate in such ventures, as the resulting exposure can greatly boost sales. If this opportunity isn't offered, you can make yourself available to local talk show hosts. But if you take the initiative, you should first make sure your book is actually available in area stores.

Autograph parties are another way to hype your book, although such projects can meet with mixed success. Contact your local bookstore if this appeals to you. Your presence may not sell enough books to greatly augment your next royalty statement, but it should stir up a little extra interest. It can also stroke your ego if enough folks ask you to autograph their copies. Of course, there's the danger of being ignored entirely, and that can be considerably less fun.

The key to continuing soul-satisfying amounts of royalty income lies in authoring books that sell long and well, and in regularly adding to the titles you have in print. The first can be accomplished by selecting subjects of widespread and long-lived appeal. Some areas of publishing are badly overworked; too many titles are available. If your work about trout fishing or raising hamsters is similar in content to another fifty or sixty books still in print, chances are against its achieving more than modest sales. And even without such competition, how many hamster lovers will be willing to part with ten dollars or so to acquire your expertise? If your audience is too narrow, there's no way your book can make either you or your publisher rich.

On the other hand, a well-written, highly publicized book about solving "The Ten Most Common" sexual problems is likely to sell well despite numerous similar titles. Self-help and how-to books are the staple of the nonfiction author—if you can find novel ways to help the reader save money, enjoy leisure time, become more attractive, improve his income, or discover any of the other pressing things we all want from life, you can probably sell a book about it. If you hit exactly the right combination at the proper time, you may have a bestseller on your hands.

Some of the most successful nonfiction books are surprisingly simple in concept. One paperback title I recall is *1001 Things You Can Get Free*. This little volume is merely a listing of government and private sources you can write to for free recipes, crop-planting advice, sample products, and the like. To date, it's enjoyed several printings and has earned its author a small fortune in royalties.

A visit to any bookstore or newsstand should give you a

rough idea of the titles being marketed. Check the current offerings and see if you can spot a hole in the lineup. What would your interests be in looking for a book to buy? Beware of following publishing fads, as these are usually short-lived. While the vanguard books on such topics as running or natural foods may sell very well, the hordes of copycats that inevitably follow are rarely as successful. By the time a new trend becomes obvious, it's usually too late to cash in on it profitably. By the time you have your follow-up book written, published, and distributed, another fad will be in vogue.

With a little careful thought and some free-running imagination, you may be the one to instigate the next hot idea. Look ahead and try to determine what activity, product, or pursuit will become popular in months ahead, and see if you can build a book proposal to profit from it. If you can sell your idea to a publisher and crank the book out in time, you could easily find yourself in an entirely new income bracket. Timing and judgment are key factors here—if you've been correct in predicting a forthcoming fad early enough to have your book in print right at the beginning, you may be very well rewarded. But don't bother chasing fads after the fact.

The best bet in developing a steady income from book royalties lies in authoring solid, well-founded books that should enjoy long publishing lives. If you produce such books regularly, before long you'll be receiving twice-yearly checks adding up to a cozy supplemental income. The fact that you have to do no further work to earn this money makes those checks even more delightful.

Writing nonfiction trade books puts the freelancer in a position similar to that enjoyed by a successful insurance agent. Each policy the agent writes produces a small but steady income as long as the client continues to pay the premiums. A book that earns royalties serves the same function—money keeps coming in as long as the public keeps buying in sufficient quantities. One book or insurance policy may not generate remarkable annual sums, but when you add the results of the years' collective efforts the numbers can wax impressive.

Of course, the book author enjoys a sizable advantage over

the insurance agent. There's no rule that says your book's income *has* to be modest. If your title catches on, a single book can make you modestly wealthy with no further effort.

However, it's unwise to count heavily on a lone title's success. Every book published constitutes a gamble, and while some few pay off, many do not. You can't stop and rest after mailing a completed manuscript while you wait for the proceeds to pour in. A true professional will have one or two (or more) other contracts already signed, with the latest books lined up and ready to be worked on. That first book is merely a foundation on which to build, and the more books you get into print, the higher your yearly income will rise. In other words, don't waste time patting yourself on the back for finishing a project. Once it's safely in the mail you should forget about it and get started on the next proposal in the hopper. A few quiet moments spent in reflection and self-congratulation may be acceptable at the completion of a months-long project, but such pleasant reveries have little cash value. Remember, time is a perishable commodity and is better spent in creative—and profitable—effort.

While long-term royalties can form a significant portion of a writer's income, don't overlook those initial cash advances. Typically, you'll receive half the agreed-upon advance immediately on signing the contract. The balance should be payable on receipt of the finished manuscript. Some publishers vary this schedule, with a third of the advance paid up front, a second third payable when half the work is completed, and the remainder due when the entire manuscript is in the publisher's hands. Another variation is for the final payment to be made on publication—a stipulation best avoided, as there can be lengthy delays between the receipt and actual publication of a book-length manuscript. As I've said before, there's no such thing as a *standard* publishing agreement, but nearly all publishers will agree to the fifty-fifty advance split. If your contract stipulates a less favorable payment arrangement, try to hold out for half the advance paid in advance, the other half due on completion of the manuscript. This is a widely accepted convention, and any significant exception should be resisted.

Some publishers may offer to publish your book without any advance or payment on their part. University presses are particularly prone to this practice, as they're used to dealing with academic authors who must "publish or perish" to maintain professorial credentials. Freelance writers must publish or perish, too, but not at the cost of writing a book on sheer speculation or without a contractual advance. If a book is worth publishing, it's worth sufficient advance payment to (at least partially) compensate the author for her time. If a publishing contract is offered *without* a respectable cash advance, my advice is to turn it down. Even a wholly untried author deserves better consideration. Freelance writing is a business, after all, and no businessperson can afford to work free.

As you can see, book-length projects are highly desirable to any freelance writer who wishes to succeed. The actual writing can be spaced out over several months and sandwiched between magazine assignments. Thus there's never any wasted time in the freelancer's schedule. If he's all caught up on his magazine writing for that month, he can turn to his book. And if he tires of that, he can take a fresh tack and get a new proposal for yet another book assembled and mailed to a prospective publisher. Effective book authorship is a never-ending enterprise. You should always have at least one book in the chute you're currently working on, another scheduled and signed, and three or four good proposals making the rounds as future possibilities.

Building a freelance career exclusively around magazine assignments is a catch-as-catch-can existence, with an income neither as substantial nor stable as book authorship brings. For the full-time freelancer, book sales are almost a necessity. Part-time writers can probably get along without this income, but there's no reason they should so handicap themselves.

Royalties are truly the freelancer's best friend. They provide the surest path to long-term self-sufficiency available to full-time writers, and can be equally rewarding to part-timers. If your book hits it big, your entire lifestyle can change overnight. Book writing is one gamble that offers excellent odds. All it requires is persistence and professionalism on the part of the author.

I've devoted the bulk of this chapter to authors of nonfiction, because nonfiction book contracts are easier to come by and generally more businesslike in approach. Novels represent greater uncertainty to publisher and author alike, but it's nonetheless a gamble that *can* yield rich results. Many novels earn no more than a first advance, but lightning sometimes strikes and big money is made. If you enjoy writing fiction and you're successful in selling a novel or two, this may be the best road for you to follow. However, the market currently reflects a buyers' preference for nonfiction books.

Whichever route you choose, you must produce consistently over several years before trying to tally the results. It takes time to build a solid income from book royalties—unless lightning and the Good Fairy both strike at once. Overnight success *can* happen, but it's best not to count on such good fortune. If you're patient and persistent, you needn't depend on luck. Build those royalties a step at a time, and you'll make your own luck in the long run.

13

Bad Times and How to Avoid (or At Least Survive) Them

Cash-flow problems are the perennial bane of the full-time freelancer. The old promise of a "check that's in the mail" (the original tall story?) holds little comfort when the mortgage payment is due, the fridge empty, and the checking account overdrawn.

If you've followed the advice I gave in chapter 10 and have six months' worth of income nestled away in a savings account and all your bills fully paid, you have no real problem—right? All you have to do is run down to the bank and make a quick withdrawal.

Would that it were so. I know from experience that most writers who turn to full-time freelancing aren't financially well-prepared for the break. They may have a few hundred bucks in savings and be up-to-date on house payments, but the majority aren't really ready for the cash-flow problems a freelancer typically faces.

Even if that part-time writing income equaled the freelancer's corporate pay before she quit, there'll be trouble ahead. In the first place, most freelancers figure income on an annual basis, averaging the good months with the bad. Unfortunately, those bad months may fall back to back, and even in a profitable year there will be periods that are mighty lean. If she has savings aplenty to fall back on, the writer need not worry. But if her savings have already been depleted and the utility company is threatening to turn off the water and gas, she has problems. Several thousand dollars "out on the books" is no solace if a check doesn't show up in next morning's mail.

Another problem is one I mentioned in an earlier chapter: Outgo inevitably rises to match income, and by the time the part-time freelancer quits her regular job her spending habits (and those of her spouse) will already have changed. In short, she's now used to a *double* income, and when she relinquishes those corporate paychecks her accustomed sustenance will be effectively cut in half.

Simple prudence would advise a reduced spending schedule any time you make a major change in your earning situation. But if you've already accumulated a sizable debt load through undisciplined credit buying, that's not going to help much. Bank credit cards may seem to offer a short-term solution to paying other bills, since you can get cash advances as long as the credit line holds out. However, funds you obtain in this manner become mighty expensive at the interest rates charged. This only adds to your monthly debt load as those cash draws are repaid. You can soon dig yourself into a hole that gets steadily deeper, and the resulting financial pressures can quickly force you back to nine-to-five employment in the company fold. Poor money management has destroyed more promising writing careers than any other single factor. Having the requisite writing talent is only part of the battle. You must be able to remain solvent until your freelance income stabilizes, and this is where so many dreams break down.

Other than borrowing at usurious interest rates or using a rob-Peter-to-pay-Paul technique to satisfy those pressing creditors, are there any other solutions a freelancer can explore? There surely are. All it takes is a little know-how and the right approach.

Aside from keeping the utilities on and food atop the table, your number-one priority should be protecting your credit rating. This means you shouldn't wait until you're several months behind in payments to take action. Once you're in that position and creditors are ringing the phone off the hook (assuming it's still connected), your credit will already have sustained a fair amount of damage.

The thing to do when payment problems threaten is immediately contact your creditors and explain your situation. Do this in person, and dress to make a businesslike impression. That means wearing the same clothes you wore at your old office job. Whatever you do, don't show up at the credit manager's office looking like the free spirit you now imagine yourself to be. Jeans and sandals are fine at home, but such attire rubs financial types the wrong way.

Explain why you're having temporary financial difficulties—and be sure to stress they're *only* temporary in nature. Any new business expects lean times at first, and your self-employed status deserves the same consideration. You are a businessperson, after all. That you're selling manuscripts rather than roller-skate wheels should have no bearing on the subject.

To back you up, bring along copies of recently published articles, written assignment confirmations from editors, and any book contracts you may have on hand. Make your presentation as impressive as possible; any evidence you can produce showing income promised or a good publishing record will help. If you have a monthly column assignment or long-standing agreement to contribute regularly to a magazine, a letter from the editor saying so can be of great value. You're trying to establish your legitimacy as a published—and still publishing—writer and convince the person you're talking to that you're a solid credit risk. If your past credit history is unblemished, you'll be on even more solid ground.

If you've presented your case at all well, you should have no trouble getting a credit manager to accept temporarily reduced payments. She might even reduce the payments permanently over a longer time until the debt is paid. As long as you're able to pay *something* on the bill every month, nearly any creditor should be willing to work with you.

If the account in question is a revolving charge account, offer assurances you won't incur further debt on that particular line of credit until you're again able to resume full-scale payments. Then be sure to keep current on the reduced payments, as promised. You may even get permission to skip one, or at the most two, payments if necessary, but most credit managers are more comfortable if *some* monthly payment is made toward your account.

By transacting such arrangements in advance—and that means *before* you're several months in arrears—you'll be able to maintain a decent credit rating while easing over a temporary rough spot. The ideal time to approach a creditor is *before* your next payment is overdue. If trouble looms on the horizon, it's best to head it off before it gets out of hand. By going to the credit manager *before* your rating is in danger, you're doing the both of you a big favor. She'll be able to carry you on the books as a current debtor in good standing, which looks good on her efficiency reports, while some of the immediate pressure will be taken off you. Whenever a debtor shows as a delinquent entry, the credit manager looks bad. So remember—it's in her interest to go along with your request if she possibly can. It's up to you to make that possibility look attractive. The fact that you came to her openly in the first place is a big point in your favor, as most real deadbeats must be pursued through letters, telephone calls, and personal visits. Treat your proposal for temporarily reduced or deferred payments as a businesslike request, and chances are excellent it will be granted. Once you've won such a concession, make sure you honor your end of the bargain fully and always on time. Such behavior will stand you in excellent stead if you ever again have similar problems. But if you renege on your agreement, your credit rating and reputation will surely suffer; such things come back to haunt you.

Another option to consider when you give up your regular job is going to your bank to establish a line of credit. Again, any credentials you show to prove you're capable of earning a satisfactory freelancing income will help. It will also help to have several hundred dollars deposited in your checking and savings accounts when you make the move. If you're obviously solvent at the time you ask for a line of credit, you stand a much better chance of receiving favorable considera-

tion than if you wait until your back is against the wall and
creditors are closing in. A bank line of credit is nothing more
than a stated sum of money the bank agrees to lend you in
months ahead. If you don't need to draw any funds against
this amount, fine—if you're lucky you won't. But if you suddenly run short, you can exercise your option to borrow any
part of the amount agreed upon. What's more, you can continue borrowing until that line of credit is exhausted. Credit of
this type is a financial tool used by many businesses, and
there's no reason you as a self-employed businessman
shouldn't take advantage of the same convention.

If you've dealt with the same bank manager over several
years, and made and retired a few auto loans or other short-
term debts, there's yet another possibility if you find yourself
in immediate need of cash. This is a signature note, so-called
because no collateral is required. Such notes normally are
issued for a thirty-, sixty-, or ninety-day period, although it's
possible to arrange a note to cover a longer time span. They're
payable in a lump sum when due, and the interest charged is
usually much lower than on a conventional installment loan.
If at the end of the period you don't have enough money to
pay the full amount owed, you can almost always pay one-
third to one-half the sum and renew the balance for an additional thirty or ninety days. I've used this kind of debt vehicle
several times when cash-flow problems (caused by overdue
checks from publishers) ran my checking account short. Depending on your current standing at the bank, it's possible to
get anywhere from $1,000 to $2,500 (or more) on the strength
of your signature alone. Just make sure you know whence—
and when—the money is coming to pay off the loan. If you're
not sure how warmly your bank manager feels toward you,
you might bring along a recent book contract or a few assignment confirmations to wave around while you negotiate the
loan.

Much of your negotiating power depends on your past relationship with the bank, and it helps a great deal if the manager knows you personally. In other words, make yourself
known well in advance, preferably while you're still safely
employed by that business. If the bank personnel perceive

you from the beginning as a solid citizen, the reputation will do no end of good when you turn to full-time freelancing.

Another source of ready cash is life-insurance loans. Many policies allow you to borrow against the cash value you've accumulated, at rates substantially lower than banks and other lending institutions offer. Your insurance agent should be able to quickly tell you if this is a viable option.

If you own a home or other real estate, it's usually possible to take out a mortgage loan against your equity in the property. This is something to be regarded as a last resort, because it reduces your net worth and the resulting monthly payments add yet another load to your struggling budget. There's also the risk of losing your home if you fail to meet the resulting payments.

Don't overlook the possibility of putting the bite on a wealthy relative if the situation warrants such action. It's much more preferable to remain independent (particularly since the relative in question may wonder aloud why you don't just find a real job), but if this is an alternative you should definitely keep it in mind. One of the advantages of such borrowing is that interest charges may be nonexistent, or at least very low. Disadvantages include being forced to listen to unwelcome if well-meant advice, and moral and financial indebtedness to family members.

Whether your new freelancing career is viewed as a credit liability or banking asset by financial managers depends partly on how you yourself regard it. If you carry an aura of confidence into your loan interview and come prepared with records of both past and expected earnings, you'll be off on the right foot. But if you walk in gloomy and insecure, you're practically begging to be turned down.

If you've established a fair earning record from your writing receipts (and you certainly shouldn't be freelancing full-time unless you have), you can use this to bolster your position as a beginning businessman with an excellent future. Income tax records, check vouchers, old contracts, and any other verification of past earnings you have can be used to put you in the best possible financial light. It's particularly helpful if these records show a substantial annual increase in freelancing income. In my own case, freelance pay took a small jump during my first full year of self-employment compared to part-time earnings the year before—but nearly doubled in the following twelve months. Such performance makes bank managers ecstatic, and if you can maintain the pace you'll be looked on as a prime credit risk. Of course, this kind of success makes it increasingly less likely you'll *need* a loan in the first place.

While obtaining short-term loans to use as operating funds can be relatively easy for the writer-businessperson who goes about it properly, qualifying for big, long-term money for new-home mortgages and the like can be entirely different.

The full-time freelancer faces several problems when she applies for a large mortgage loan. In the first place, she's suspect as a self-employed person—and the fact that she's a writer rather than a brick manufacturer or carpetlayer only adds further uncertainty. Any self-employed person, unless wildly successful and very obviously well-fixed, is viewed with skepticism by mortgage-loan officers because of difficulty verifying employment and income. The majority of bank customers hold down regular jobs; all that's needed to verify employment is a phone call to the personnel director. "Yes, Manfred has been a faithful employee for the past sixteen years. That's right—his annual earnings total $22,012.26. And his prospects are excellent."

When a self-employed person applies for a mortgage loan, the officer is placed in the position of accepting the applicant's word with regard to annual income. And even if you made good money last year, the mortgage company would feel better if it had positive assurances your business will continue to be healthy. If you worked for a large, long-established company with hundreds or thousands of employees, the agency would feel fairly confident your source of employment wouldn't dry up and disappear overnight. The agency feels decidedly less secure when dealing with self-employed writers. People who earn their livings through creative endeavor are obvious nonconformists, and rate low marks for dependability as far as most financial institutions are concerned. When you become as well known as Capote or

Wambaugh, you can literally name your own terms to fawn-
ing loan officers. But until that happens, you'll be fighting an
uphill battle when big money is needed.

Of course, no mortgage-loan officer is about to take your
word for claimed income, and here lies another stumbling
block to receiving your loan. The criteria generally accepted
from the self-employed are copies of old income tax returns
for the last several years. The only figures moneylenders
count are the net income totals you actually pay taxes on.
This is where many freelancers come to grief.

Most full-time freelancers take so many tax deductions
that reported business gross and personal net income may be
kilometers, if not miles, apart. A writer who earns $40,000 a
year for his work may whittle that down to $25,000 or less for
taxpaying purposes, and it's the latter figure the mortgage
loan people look at. Since most such organizations are loathe
to lend more than two or two-and-a-half times your available
annual income for *any* purpose, you can only borrow a fraction of the amount you would qualify for if *gross* income
could be used. That means you may not qualify for a large
enough loan to buy that dream house, although you actually
earn enough to easily handle the payments.

I ran into that very problem recently, and this is how I
solved it: Because the taxable income shown on my return
forms was considerably lower than my actual yearly gross, I
had the mortgage company contact all the editors I regularly
write for. They supplied figures to show the amount each had
paid me to date for the current year. The mortgage people
then extrapolated these figures (which covered the first seven
months of the year) into a probable annual payment total.
Magazines with which I had contractual agreements to do a
certain amount of writing supplied the information, and *this*
payment was added in. Then I produced the book contracts I
had signed during the year, and *their* advances were included
in the total. By the time everything was added together, I
qualified handily for a substantial first mortgage loan. If necessary, book-royalty statements could have pushed the total
higher.

Incidentally, it's wise to telephone each of the editors involved in such an impromptu survey to make sure they know exactly why the information is needed. Contact them before they receive queries from the mortgage company, and tell them what's happening. Most editors will be happy to comply with your request, and will feel better about releasing financial information if they know you've sanctioned the query.

Once you've freelanced full-time for several years, you can compile a solid history of annual earnings. If your income shows steady growth, the information will warm any bank manager's heart next time you need a short-term loan. Spectacular growth is even better, and this can be a distinct possibility when you freelance for a living.

There's a widespead assumption that anyone engaged in a business as obviously risky as freelance writing has almost no financial security. Some freelancers themselves feel this way, and this is one reason so many ultimately fail to make a full-time career of writing. The fact is, a competent freelancer can enjoy more security than her corporate-job-holding counterpart. An employee can lose her job for a number of reasons. If that happens, her income is completely cut off (except for unemployment benefits) until she finds another job. What's more, hunting another position can take several months and the unlucky ex-employee may in the end have to accept a lower-paying job.

If a freelancer writer gets "fired" by an editor, it should be less of a calamity. Most magazine writers contribute to several different publications on a more-or-less regular basis, and the loss of a single market results in the loss of only a portion of the usual monthly income. This loss can be quickly made up as another editor starts buying. If the writer has a couple of book projects in the works, chances are the dissenting editor will hardly be missed.

During a particularly bad spell during my first year as a full-time freelancer, my bank manager actually discouraged me from returning to corporate employment. He pointed out that my writing and manuscript sales record showed it was unlikely the dry spell would last, and he encouraged me to stick it out by extending a fresh line of credit. He also reminded me that working for a company would never make me rich, as each salary increase would largely be nullified by the rising cost of living. As a self-employed freelancer I might never attain real fame or fortune, either, but at least there was an outside chance of one or the other happening.

Because the potential rewards for freelancing are so great, the full-time writer just starting out should do everything possible to see that the career isn't shortstopped by financial trouble. This requires some early adjustment in spending habits and a budget flexible enough to accommodate the peaks and valleys typical of a freelancer's cash flow. A sizable savings account is the best backup for the months checks are slow to come in, but a good credit rating and friendly bank manager are also excellent assets.

If you'll view your professional writing career as the legitimate business enterprise it is, you should have no qualms seeking short-term financial aid if this becomes necessary. Full-time freelancers constitute no greater loan risk than other self-employed businessmen, and with the proper approach you should have little trouble qualifying for credit. Just make sure you don't abuse such credit when offered, and do all you can to keep your creditors happy. If you encounter unexpected problems, let them know before your payments fall past due.

However, borrowing money for operating funds is strictly a stopgap measure to be considered only in a genuine emergency. Indebtedness has a sneaky way of piling up, and if the debts grow too large your *real* troubles are just beginning. So manage your money wisely, and budget carefully. Pickings might be slim the first year or a bit longer, but if you have the necessary drive you'll soon be back on a steak-and-mushroom diet for keeps. So don't give up too soon. With the right attitude and a little planning and preparation, you should weather those early financial crises. And if a crisis never occurs, you can rest easy in the knowledge that you're nonetheless prepared.

14

The Good Times (When It All Seems Worthwhile)

While full-time freelancers face a number of common problems when starting out, a successful freelance writing career is perhaps the most enviable of occupations. Your income is limited only by your own drive and ability, and you have more personal freedom than almost anyone in town.

As a self-employed writer, you're likely to find yourself working harder than ever before. Professional writing *is* hard work, make no mistake about that. Creating entertaining and informative copy that's up to publishable standards is a surprisingly difficult chore, and when you have to meet tight deadlines the pressure can become enormous. Tackling a book-length project with the delivery date only a few months away seems an awesome task, and committing yourself to writing columns or feature articles for a particular magazine on a monthly basis demands awful discipline. When the resulting pay is slow coming in, you can become disheartened and discouraged.

No, as a full-time freelancer you'll work harder and longer hours than you'd bargained for. If deadline looms and your work is undone, you may spend a stretch of sixteen hours at the typewriter. Most writers I know work almost all the time. Even at the dinner table or driving to the beach, their brains are turning over article ideas. Writing isn't something you turn off when you cover your typewriter and leave the office. If you're not consciously working on some writing project, you can bet the old subconscious is still cranking away. As many writers can testify, this process continues during sleep. I can't count the times I've gone to bed wondering how to handle a topic, and woke up next morning eager to pound the keys. Some of those pieces literally wrote themselves, and I felt like bylining my subconscious as coauthor.

When you leave the nine-to-five schedule of corporate employment to freelance full-time, you lose the luxury of earning your living in a mere eight hours a day. The most important work is done in a writer's head; there's a part of your mind always tuned to the manuscript next due. Getting your thoughts on paper obviously is important, but this is just the mechanical part of the job. The real tool is your brain.

Despite all this effort, the writing life is still marvelous to contemplate. Your working hours are decided by you alone, and can change whenever you desire. Most truly successful writers maintain a daily writing discipline, and some keep hours as rigid as any deskbound accountant or office clerk; some writers find that as long as they put four or five hours in at the typewriter each day, it doesn't matter when those hours are scheduled. Consequently, they feel free to answer daily moods or whims. If a walk in the woods sounds attractive or you decide to take a shopping trip downtown, no one is going to yell at you if you drop your work in mid-paragraph and take a few hours off—or even the rest of the day. You may have to pay for too many such indulgences later, as you can't push back fixed publishing deadlines. If you play hooky from the keyboard all day, you'll probably have to put in longer stints the following days to keep on schedule. Nonetheless, such freedom is highly enjoyable, and sure to be envied by less liberated folk.

The freedom from clock alarms is another to be treasured. For far too many years I was jolted from bed by the alarm's harsh clangor at an ungodly six o'clock, in order to wipe the sleep from my eyes, dress, and drive forty-six miles to my office. (I showered and shaved before bed to squeeze an extra quarter-hour of sleep from each morning's frantic schedule— skipped breakfast, too.)

Six o'clock may not sound terrible to those raised on a farm, but to a city-bred lad like myself it's a horrible time to start the day. The sun isn't even up at that hour a good part of the year, and I've always figured that if God had intended for us to be up and moving around in the dark we'd have been born with flashlights in our skulls. The predawn winter hours are not a pleasant time to face rush-hour traffic on the inter- state.

The first thing I did on becoming a certified self-employed writer was remove the arming switch on my bedside clock. I now rise around eight, when I once would have been groping about my desk a few cities away. By eight o'clock, two of my three children have been up, showered, fed, and packed off to school, and it's this commotion that usually rouses me to wakefulness. If not, I sleep blissfully on, although I'm almost always up and writing by nine.

Other freelancers I know are habitual early risers and may be hammering at their typewriters hours before dawn. Their working day is likely to finish before lunchtime if they're not behind schedule, and they have the whole afternoon to play. And don't think I use the word "play" in jest. Play is impor- tant for both children and adults, although many of us lose sight of this. Our lives are so structured by the usual working and living environment that most grownups have very little time left each day for honest relaxation. And if we do try to squeeze in a few sets of tennis before or after dinner, the courts are filled with others who had the same idea. In a society where everyone quits work at five, leisure activities are limited by available time and playing space.

By contrast, the writer can use public recreation areas at almost any time; most public courts aren't crowded at two on Tuesday afternoon. The main problem lies in finding a tennis, swimming, or golf partner who enjoys similar freedom.

The ability to structure your life to please yourself alone is a precious one, much appreciated by the creative types most likely to turn to writing or art as a full-time occupation. The resulting self-responsibility can be frightening, but if you're mature enough to properly balance your time between work and play it's a great way to live.

Married couples without children have almost unlimited mobility, as the necessary writing can be done from a motel room, tent, or pickup camper. I know of several husband-wife writing teams who travel continually, earning their way as they go. The nomadic life can be addictive; freelancers have this option open.

The full-time freelancer generally finds family life enhanced, as he or she can always make time for children or spouse. If the children have a day free from school, a writer can take a holiday himself and the whole family can do something fun and different (assuming that the spouse also has a flexible schedule). When Christmas vacation rolls around, you can take extra days off instead of rushing back to the office on December 26. Summer picnics and fishing trips can be planned on the spur of the moment, and longer journeys can be almost equally impromptu. One of the most memorable vacations my family has had was thrown together overnight when a book contract put several thousand dollars unexpectedly at hand the week after school finished for the summer. On an impulse, we decided to blow most of the money on a first-class family outing rather than sensibly put it in savings. Two days later we were en route to California, where my wife, three teenage sons, and I did the whole Disneyland and studio-tour bit. When we wandered south from Los Angeles and discovered a particularly delightful beachfront hotel, we simply stretched our vacation another four days to lie on the sand and soak up sun. Since we simply decided to go and didn't have to plan months ahead to fit a company vacation roster, it was even more fun. And when we decided to stay nearly another week, that option was open. When we finally returned home, I had to work overtime to meet a few threatening deadlines, but other than that the trip created no strain.

Another fringe benefit a writer may find is all-expense-paid travel in the U.S. or abroad. This depends partly on the publications you write for and the assignments you draw, but many freelancers enjoy frequent travel. If this possibility interests you, try writing travel features for your local newspaper and other likely markets. The rates you'll be paid for newspaper freelancing won't help you much toward your monthly earnings goal, but if you find travel interesting a few published pieces can open the door to offers from airlines, foreign chambers of commerce, and other agencies interested in publicizing their services.

You don't have to qualify as "travel writer" to roam abroad, either. Hunting and fishing writers spend a good share of time out of the country, and if you're involved in product testing and review you may be invited to visit the facilities of a foreign manufacturer. All expenses are taken care of on such trips, of course, and you usually travel first class. Many different types of writers find reason to travel abroad, often at little or no cost to their own pocketbooks.

I personally don't do anything that could be classified as travel writing, yet in the last two years I've visited Spain, Italy, Mexico, Germany, and Finland with stops in other countries en route. I stayed at least a week in each country, and had to diet between trips to rid myself of pounds gained eating at four-star restaurants along the way. These trips cost me nothing other than what I spent for souvenirs. What's more, I turned down offers for at least two other excursions. If I stopped to figure what I would have spent traveling on my own funds, I could say I've lived a pretty rich life recently. Such travel can be considered a freelancer's fringe benefit— yet another reason many writers earn the envy of their "straight" working neighbors.

Even if you do dig into your own pocket for travel, chances are you can find a way to turn each trip into a legitimate tax deduction. Obviously you can't write off family vacation trips, but when you're doing field research for magazine assignments or gathering background material and color for a novel, you're usually justified in letting Uncle Sam help foot the bill. These trips still draw your checking account down, but at least you can get some rebate on April 15.

Another benefit writers often receive is monies which arrive in hefty lump sums. While magazine articles may furnish your day-to-day income, book contracts can generate advances running several thousand dollars a crack, and when royalties are paid twice each year the checks can be impressive. I have a freelancing friend who pays cash for a new automobile each year from one of his several summer royalty payments. Getting your hands on large chunks of change periodically gives you this advantage over your nonwriting friends: By buying cars or large appliances outright, you can save greatly in interest charges over the year. It also helps not to have those nasty monthly payments to make.

Of course, there's always the fact that your income is essentially unlimited. The amount of money you're able to earn each year is dependent totally on you and what you do. If you work very hard and sell to the right markets, you can have a fantastic year financially. This is a sword that cuts both ways, but if you're willing to seriously apply yourself it's possible to collect an eminently enviable income. If you're fortunate enough to write a best-selling book, you can quickly advance through the upper-middle class to the ranks of the nouveaux riches. While that possibility may be slim, it exists—which is more than the typical office worker can even hope for.

While potential financial rewards and a high degree of personal freedom are considerable pluses in the freelancer's life, writers also receive great satisfaction because their work is read by hundreds of thousands, even millions, of people each month. The importance of what you think or say is thus magnified by the medium in which your writing appears. You have a personal impact on society, and this can be extremely satisfying to the ego.

What's more, you can see tangible results of your efforts on a regular, continuing basis. Your byline appears in national and regional magazines, and your name is included in the authors' listing at the Library of Congress. You can see what you've done simply by visiting the local newsstand. Contrast this with the lot of most corporate employees. They make significant contributions to the economy, but there's little apparent evidence to the fact. There's scarce satisfaction to be gained in assembly-line work, cashiering at a grocery counter, or stocking shelves. Office workers also operate in little-varied day-to-day routines that show but small personal achievement. The "people behind the scenes" are legion, but publishing writers can legitimately view themselves as a breed apart. Few full-time freelancers suffer problems stemming from underdeveloped egos. It takes a certain self-confidence to even try to make a living as a writer, and those who succeed are likely to emerge with a strong sense of self-worth.

If you write long enough for the same publications, your name becomes familiar to a surprising number of people. If your photo appears with any regularity, you may even be recognized at the supermarket twice a year. If you're a writer living in a small community, you may become a mini-celebrity in time. Such public recognition is hardly a constant occurrence for most freelance writers, but when it happens it can brighten your day considerably. Sometimes such recognition carries unexpected benefits. My eldest son was recently stopped for speeding by an out-of-state trooper. He was driving my car at the time, and when he handed over the registration papers the patrolman did a double take. It turned out he was a fan of mine (he subscribed to a magazine I write a column for), and ended up waving my son on his way. That policeman may have been the only person in all Idaho who knew my name, but he did and it made an indelible impression on my son. He regarded me with increased respect for nearly a full hour after returning home. Fleeting as such fame is, it's fun when it happens.

As you become better known, you can even look forward to a smattering of fan mail. Magazines forward letters addressed to you care of them, and once in a while a reader will learn your phone number and call. This can he heady stuff indeed, but the praise you thus receive should never be taken too seriously. Still, it's flattering to know someone enjoyed reading your material enough to tell you so.

I understand many unattached freelancers extract a bit of social mileage from writing as an occupation. Being introduced as a writer at a party imparts an aura of minor glamor; people regard you with some awe. Writers are equated in a small way with the Hemingways and Faulkners of the world, and what freelancer is going to take many pains to dispel this notion? That he is merely a staff writer for an obscure industrial magazine rather than a successful novelist or screenwriter may not come to light. What man is going to make such a confession to the silly but gorgeous girl who's all aquiver at meeting an in-the-flesh literary lion? What female freelancer would admit to writing Gothic potboilers when mistaken for another Joyce Carol Oates?

The *real* reason writing is the most enviable of all occupations is that you truly enjoy the time you spend at that typewriter. If you *don't* find pleasure in creating manuscripts or communicating in print, for heaven's sake don't try to make your living at this trade! Most professional writers I know are inwardly driven to write. They'd do it as a hobby if they couldn't be paid, and their ability to earn good money doing what they like is regarded as an unbelievable bonus. This is the final reward: the ability to do what you really want to do, and to make your full living at it. Part-time writers sip this heady brew, but the full-time freelancer quaffs it daily and to the dregs. Real writers simply love to write. It can be hard, tiring work, but that makes it no less gratifying. Too few people are truly satisfied with their lifetime occupations, but I've never met a freelancer who wasn't. As one writer once told me, "I'm having so much fun, getting paid for what I'm doing should be illegal!" That's the real payoff—the one that counts.

15

The Writer and Society (What Will the Neighbors Think?)

When you take up freelancing as a full-time career, there are social adjustments you, your spouse, and the neighbors will have to make. Some of these you may have been wise enough to foresee, but others will come as a complete surprise.

Unless you live in New York City or Los Angeles, where deviant behavior is the norm and writers and artists are accepted as commonplace, your neighbors will have a hard time accepting your new freelance status. That's a promise. This phenomenon is particularly true if the writer is the head of the family, although single writers come in for their fair share of social abuse.

A husband and father who turns to writing full-time is viewed with a mixture of sympathy and suspicion by those who live next door or across the street. The first reaction is invariably, "The poor guy's lost his job and is trying to maintain a brave front." This results in well-meaning offers to introduce him to the "right people" at various businesses, and hot meals are likely to be delivered to the door. As your "unemployment" stretches from weeks to months, the neighbors become increasingly distressed. Pointed questions of "How're things going?" will be asked at every meeting, as your friends narrow their eyes in concern. If you counter this solicitude by patiently explaining your newfound career, and even mention the book contract you've signed, they're still apt to walk off shaking their heads and clucking in sympathy.

If you prosper and do something ostentatious like buying a new car, many neighbors will view this as whistling in the dark. However, if the car you buy is a bit *too* nice, other acquaintances will begin to wonder if you're perpetrating welfare fraud. Even if you eventually convince those who live near you that you're really earning a living writing, normal people will find it difficult to accept your presence at home. God-fearing folk with legitimate jobs all tear off for the office at eight o'clock and have the decency to stay away until just before suppertime. If you don't fit this commuter mold, you're askew from the rest of the world. Anyone who dares not conform will naturally be regarded with a degree of suspicion.

The mass social consciousness has trouble comprehending those who swerve too far from the norm. For a family man to live and work at home all day is beyond ken. This is another reason many freelancers eventually rent an office downtown. I know when I did, the entire neighborhood heaved a subconscious sigh of relief. Since I could be observed leaving for "work" most mornings, and I stayed away most of the day, it was obvious I was gainfully employed once again. That I made it clear I was still fully self-employed made no difference. I had someplace to go every day, and that made me safe once again. The pressure was off, and neighbors no longer pestered my wife and children: "Has he found work yet?"

A writer/homemaker causes no such concern on the part of the neighborhood coffee klatsch. As long as the children look clean and neat when they head to school and meals are ostensibly served properly, few people care what the woman of the house does with her spare time. Working wives who freelance part-time have a problem unless the husband pitches in and does his share of the housework. This is a more equitable arrangement in any case, but is particularly important when part-time writing is used to expand the budget. Freelancing is regarded as a perfectly acceptable pastime, and even a woman who writes a bestselling novel is approved as long as the household chores get done.

On the other hand, a woman alone who freelances for a living may raise a few eyebrows if she stays home all day. Her lack of a visible means of support (I've always loved that phrase—does it mean no wires are showing?) can start tongues wagging.

Actually, the first year you try freelancing full-time is the worst for your neighbors and family. They'll eventually adjust to your freedom from a rigid schedule—and when this happens you can expect other problems. You may become the neighborhood handyman or taxi service—at least in the eyes of the families living around you. If your children want to head to the mountains for a day of skiing, guess who's elected to perform chauffeur duties? If you're the only parent who isn't "at work," you're the logical candidate—right? So you end up driving your children and their friends various and sundry places all year long. That is, unless you smarten up and put your foot down. The neighbors cannot comprehend that your time is worth real money, and a suggestion that Tom or Linda take a turn toting the neighborhood offspring around is likely to be met with a surprised, "But they're *working!*"

Freelancers are likely to be tabbed to write the church newsletter or spend effort in similar "literary" endeavors. People just cannot take freelance writers seriously until they achieve considerable fame. When this happens, others realize you're a real professional. But until that best seller hits the stands, you'll have an uphill battle winning much local acceptance. Don't let it bother you, and keep right on writing.

Another minor annoyance you're liable to face when word gets around you're a publishing writer is being asked to read and comment on manuscripts written by any number of would-be authors. These range from so-so pieces your niece's high-school English teacher raved about to maudlin garbage from the aging widower down the street. Critiquing manuscripts for relatives and neighbors is a no-win situation—if you're brutally honest, you can make lifelong enemies. And it's not really fair to encourage an obviously untalented writer in his or her folly. Some such requests are impossible to sidestep gracefully, and these you must handle as you best see fit. Remember, novice writers are notoriously thin-skinned, and young egos particularly fragile. Offer whatever helpful advice you can, but try to be positive with any criticisms made. Be gentle.

While close friends and family members can be difficult to turn down, more casual acquaintances are easier to handle. Explain that you're months behind schedule and that you don't really have time to give the offered masterpiece the attention it deserves. Another alternative is to express joy at the opportunity, but let slip that you charge fifty dollars an hour for your professional reading services. Then ask for an advance retainer fee. If the writer becomes indignant, ask if he gets free medical advice from his physician, or if his attorney is willing to work on that basis. Like doctors and lawyers, you're a professional. As such, you're entitled to money for services rendered.

Similarly, you may be asked to speak at various ladies' guild or Kiwanis club luncheons. A few invitations each year can be fun to honor; it gives you an excuse to leave the typewriter and associate briefly with a variety of people. Speaking at such functions offers relief from daily routine, but if the invitations become too numerous and cut into your production time, charge a lecture fee. This can range from fifty dollars up (well-known writers charge twenty to thirty times that), depending on what the market will bear and how badly you want to sidestep the invitation. Or say you'll be busy on the day selected.

While there are a few social adjustments any writer must make when she gives up her old nine-to-five job to turn to freelancing full-time, these are mostly minor. As a full-time writer, you enter the ranks of a select minority. Writers are looked upon as real oddities by average working folk. You're outside the normal range of understanding, and people don't know how to deal with your peculiar situation. For this reason, when you discover another full-time writer living nearby (anywhere within a fifty-mile radius), the two of you are likely to become close friends. Freelance artists share similar problems, and they too are members of the Family.

The initial period of adjustment is the hardest—those first several months when the neighbors discover you're no longer commuting, or when your friends are sure you're out of work and too proud to ask for help. Once you manage to convince everyone you're both happily and gainfully employed, the battle is half over. And when you finally trade your five-year-old Chevy in for a Porsche or Mercedes, the other half of the battle will be won. From then on, your most serious social difficulties are more apt to stem from jealousy than sympathy.

INDEX

107; schedule, 16-17, 128,
136-138, 143-144, 156, 171-
174; skills, 1, 9-12, 15-16,

18-19, 33, 54-55, 57, 63, 84,
86, 89, 98, 123, 135

Other Writer's Digest Books

Market Books
Artist's Market, 540 pp. $11.95
Craftworker's Market, 696 pp. $12.95
Photographer's Market, 640 pp. $12.95
Songwriter's Market, 504 pp. $11.95
Writer's Market, 936 pp. $15.95

General Writing Books
Beginning Writer's Answer Book, 264 pp. $8.95
Creative Writer, 416 pp. $8.95
Law and the Writer, 240 pp. $9.95
Make Every Word Count, 256 pp. $10.95
Treasury of Tips for Writers, 174 pp. $7.95
Writer's Resource Guide, 488 pp. $12.95

Magazine/News Writing
Complete Guide to Marketing Magazine Articles, 248 pp. $8.95
Craft of Interviewing, 244 pp. $9.95
Magazine Writing: The Inside Angle, 256 pp. $10.95
Magazine Writing Today, 220 pp. $9.95
1001 Article Ideas, 270 pp. $10.95
Stalking the Feature Story, 310 pp. $9.95
Writing and Selling Non-Fiction, 317 pp. $10.95

Fiction Writing
Handbook of Short Story Writing, 238 pp. $9.95
How to Write Short Stories that Sell, 228 pp. $9.95
One Way to Write Your Novel, 138 pp. $8.95
Secrets of Successful Fiction, 119 pp. $8.95
Writing Popular Fiction, 232 pp. $8.95
Writing the Novel: From Plot to Print, 197 pp. $10.95

Category Writing Books
Cartoonist's and Gag Writer's Handbook, (paper), 157 pp. $8.95
Confession Writer's Handbook, 200 pp. $8.95
Guide to Greeting Card Writing, 256 pp. $10.95
Guide to Writing History, 258 pp. $8.50
Mystery Writer's Handbook, 273 pp. $8.95
The Poet and the Poem, 399 pp. $11.95
Poet's Handbook, 288 pp. $10.95
Scriptwriter's Handbook, 256 pp. $10.95
Sell Copy, 224 pp. $11.95
Successful Outdoor Writing, 244 pp. $11.95
Travel Writer's Handbook, 288 pp. $11.95
Writing and Selling Science Fiction, 191 pp. $8.95
Writing for Children & Teenagers, 256 pp. $9.95
Writing for Regional Publications, 203 pp. $11.95

The Writing Business

How to Be a Successful Housewife/Writer, 254 pp. $10.95
How You Can Make $20,000 a Year Writing: No Matter Where You
Live, 270 pp. (cloth) $10.95; (paper) $6.95
Jobs For Writers, 256 pp. $10.95
Profitable Part-time/Full-time Freelancing, 256 pp. $10.95
Writer's Digest Diary, 114 pp. $9.95

To order directly from the publisher, include $1.25 postage and handling for 1-2 books; for 3 or more books, include an additional 25¢ for each book. Allow 30 days for delivery.

For a current catalog of books for writers or information on *Writer's Digest* magazine, *Writer's Yearbook*, Writer's Digest School correspondence courses or manuscript criticism, write to:

Writer's Digest Books, Department B
9933 Alliance Road, Cincinnati OH 45242

Prices subject to change without notice.